Y0-BRT-303

SECRETS of
THE CHINESE
DRAMA

To MEI LAN-FANG
WITHOUT WHOSE INSTRUCTION
THIS UNDERTAKING WOULD
HAVE BEEN IMPOSSIBLE

俏齡先生 惠存

梅蘭芳敬贈

Frontispiece

MEI LAN-FANG

Frontispiece

Mei Lan-fang in the Rôle of Hung-sien

PLAY: *The Heroic Maid*

Secrets of the Chinese Drama

A COMPLETE EXPLANATORY GUIDE TO
ACTIONS AND SYMBOLS AS SEEN IN THE
PERFORMANCE OF CHINESE DRAMAS

by CECILIA S. L. ZUNG

With Synopses of Fifty Popular Chinese Plays

and 240 illustrations.

ARNO PRESS

A New York Times Company
New York • 1980

FERNALD LIBRARY
COLBY-SAWYER COLLEGE
NEW LONDON, N.H. 03257

PL
2357
28

5/81 25.00

82587

Reprint Edition 1980 by Arno Press Inc.
First published, 1937
Reissued 1964 by Benjamin Blom, Inc.

LC 80-1696
ISBN 0-405-09112-5
Manufactured in the United States of America

Ch'êng Yen-ts'iu's Writing

A Foreword of Explanation

IF I remember rightly, I was taken to the theatre when I was a child not more than four years old. My interest in the Chinese drama has grown with my years. No matter how heavy my day's programme has been I fall under the spell of good plays, especially those in which a "tan" (see p. 37) takes the leading part. Though my friends are not surprised to hear me boasting that there is not a single play in the repertoire of Mei Lan-fang (梅蘭芳), China's most famous female impersonator, and his pupil, Ch'êng Yen-ts'iu (程硯秋), which I have not seen, yet they do reprimand me for being so foolish as to continue attending the same performances by the same actors.

   With such fondness for the theatre I would have written earlier on Chinese drama had I not been overcome by the great difficulty of putting into a foreign language the complicated technique of acting on the Chinese stage, and the feeling of my lack in literary style. To

ix

the best of my knowledge no one else has attempted to interpret in English the Chinese stage technique. And now, it is only through the strong encouragement and help of interested friends that I have ventured to undertake this work.

Here I wish to make the following acknowledgments and explanations:

1. Most of the material in Part II has been collected by Professor J. S. Chi (齊 如 山), but the gestures were personally demonstrated for me by Mei Lan-fang.

2. Dr. Mei has kindly permitted me to use his pictures to illustrate some of the more interesting movements. In addition there are some other movements interpreted by other artists and by myself.

3. I desire to express my gratitude to the firm of T. Chuang, Architects, Shanghai, for the theatre plans (see pp. 7-13) which they have drawn for me.

4. The pictures of the musical instruments, stage properties, and painted-faces are reprinted by courtesy of Professor Chi.

5. Because of the unusual length and scope of the technique of Chinese drama it is impractical to treat the subject as a whole. Therefore, I have chosen to emphasize "tan" only, the rôle in which I am particularly interested.

6. My hearty thanks are due Professor Lelia J. Tuttle and Miss Jean F. Craig for their indispensable help in the choice of English phrase and idiom, and Dr. Mei and Professor Chi for leading me into a deeper study of the technique of Chinese drama.

CECILIA S. L. ZUNG.

程 修 齡

Shanghai, China, December, 1936.

$\mathscr{P}$reface

THE English reading public will certainly greet the appearance of this book on Chinese drama with a warm welcome. The subject dealt with is very interesting, and at the same time very intricate. To the uninitiated foreigner, his first experience in a Chinese theatre will probably be intensely fascinating. But the peculiarities and strangeness which produce the charm, create also an atmosphere of bewilderment. Intelligent appreciation, which gives real delight, will come only when he shall have had his first lessons in Chinese drama, and shall have thus acquired a knowledge of the basic principles guiding the Chinese playwright and the essential features controlling stage production.

In setting, plot, and technique, the Chinese drama differs in many respects from that given on the stage of western countries. One fundamental conception to be noted at the very outset is the fact that the Chinese drama is thought of as having a higher mission than merely to entertain and amuse. It therefore appeals not only to the senses, but seeks also through the avenue of thought and reflection, to expound the meaning of life. The moral is one of the most important elements as well as one of the most prominent features of a Chinese drama. With this thought in mind, one can understand and probably even appreciate the setting and general atmosphere of the Chinese stage.

To a person visiting the Chinese theatre for the first time some of the features may appear to be primitive and absurd. In the waving of a little whip one is supposed to see the actor riding and guiding his imaginary horse. In certain motions of the hands one is to see him knocking at a make-believe door and pushing it open. There is so much of imagination and so little of reality. So many of the actions are symbolic and so few of the properties are real! But Chinese drama does not strive to be real in its physical presentation, since it is more to instruct than to amuse.

Again a person may fail to understand why there should be so much noise and confusion—the loud clanging of the gong, the sharp rattle of the flat drum, the dull clicking beat of the wooden castanets. Above these we hear the piercing sound of the Peking violin, and the falsetto soprano voice of the singing actor. So much noise, and so much confusion! Yet is it not true to life that when we think and reflect we have to lift our thoughts above the din of worldly noise? But these intricacies, differences, absurdities, noises, motifs, and technique, all resolve themselves into an intelligible artistic integrated whole as the author proceeds sympathetically and understandingly through the pages of her book.

But amateur though she may be, a real expert she nevertheless is in the realm of Chinese drama. Ever since her childhood days she has been interested in plays and later, has often demonstrated her ability in dramatic performances, both in Chinese and in English. She is familiar with both types of drama. Furthermore, as a writer in English the author distinguished herself even in her student days. She is, therefore, not only well qualified to write on the subject, but what she writes should also be well presented.

If a few more personal observations may be permitted, let it be said that the appearance of this book is significant in two other respects. It shows, in the first place, the versatility of the author, the broad cultural basis and wide interest of the new scholar in China. Professional persons are often so much engrossed in their own professions as not to be interested in other things. The author of this book has not forgotten that an educated person is one who not only aspires to know everything about something but also strives to know something about everything.

It is also significant, in the second place, in that it shows the capacity and activity of the new woman of China.

It certainly gives me great pleasure to write this short preface for a book produced by one of our graduates who is surely emerging into prominence both as a lawyer as well as writer.

Y. C. YANG.

President's Office,
  Soochow University,
    Soochow, China.

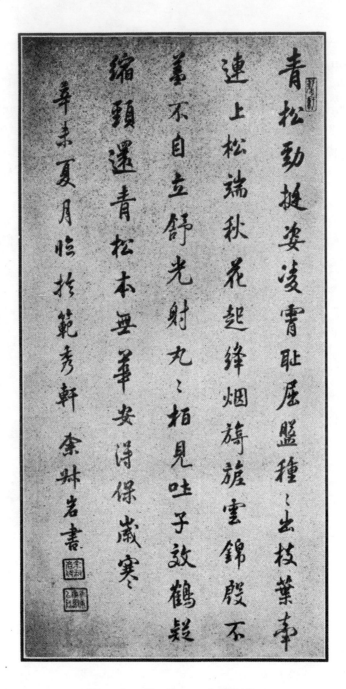

青松勁挺姿　凌霄耻屈盤　種種出枝葉幸
連上松端秋　花起鋒烟旆旒靈錦殿不
蓋不自立舒光射丸丸相見吐子效鶴毿
縮頸還青松本無華安得保歳寒

辛未夏月臨於範秀軒　余叔岩書

Illus. 1.　Yu Shu-yen's Writing

Contents

PART III. CLASSIFICATION AND SYNOPSES OF PLAYS

CONTENTS—*continued*

Page

xvii

CONTENTS—*continued*

List of Illustrations

Illus. 2. Mei Lan-fang's Painting

Mei Lan-fang's Painting

Biographical Sketch of Mei Lan-fang

Two external influences were powerful in moulding the genius of Mei Lan-fang: the musical environment of Peking (now Peiping) and the Movement for the Emancipation of Women (婦女解放運動). By the first was developed his highly aesthetic talent for drama; by the help of the second was accomplished the leadership of "tan" (the female rôle, see p. 37).

His grandfather, Mei Chiao-lin (梅巧玲), was an imperial court actor and the Director of the Peking Szu-hsi Dramatic Training School (四喜班). His father having died a very young man, the child was reared by his paternal uncle, Mei Yu-tien (梅雨田), a famous performer on the "hu-ch'in" (the Chinese violin, see p. 31, Item 3). This musical atmosphere may have played a large part in making the artist what he is today.

In real life woman was considered inferior to man, and this attitude was reflected on the stage. Those who played "chin-i," the rôle for a virtuous woman (see p. 37), were placed in the fourth rank, whereas "lao-shên," the players of aged masculine rôles (see p. 37), occupied the foremost position. Then, when woman's struggle for equality won a great number of sympathizers, the movement exerted no less influence on the stage than it had on real life: the leadership of "tan" had become possible. Above all forces contributing to Mei Lan-fang's success, however, are the upright character and the indefatigable effort of the artist himself.

On October 22, 1894, the historic city of Peking became the birthplace of the great artist. Though Mei Lan-fang was only eleven years of age when he made his first stage appearance, yet he so impressed the fastidious connoisseurs that they assured his uncle that the little man was a piece of "jadestone worthy to be fashioned and polished." They also foretold that if he were properly trained he would achieve a brilliant career. Their prophecy was soon fulfilled; his first visit to Shanghai in 1913 was such a marked success that on his return to Peking he began to be ranked above "lao-shên." Since 1917 Mei Lan-fang has been—and still is—peerless in the dramatic world of China.

Though he had never been an actor of the Imperial Court, Mei Lan-fang was granted an audience in the Yang Sing Hall (養 性 殿) of the Forbidden City by the ex-emperor, Hsüan-t'ung (宣 統), who not only presented him with some rare porcelains but made him head of the Tsing Chung Temple (精 忠 廟), which title according to the Manchu custom was the highest honour an actor could acquire.

He has produced a great number of new plays based on classical literature, and having either historical background or ethical teaching as the motive. His greatest contribution to the Chinese drama is his revival of the ancient classical dances, such as:

(a) Sword Dance in "The Final Parting between the King, P'a Wang, and His Favourite" (Illus. 69, 71)
"The Heroic Maid" (frontispiece)
"The Filial Daughter, Lien Chin-fêng" (Illus. 47)

(b) Sleeve Dance (Illus. 37)
Tray and Winepot Dance (Illus. 77) } in "Ma-ku Offering Birthday Greetings"

(c) Spear Dance in "The Rainbow Pass" (Illus. 82, 83)

(d) Fan Dance (Illus. 81)
Flute and Plume Dance (Illus. 80) } in "The Patriotic Beauty, Hsi Shih"

His performances have attracted crowded audiences not only of his own countrymen but of foreign spectators as well. He has been requested to visit a number of foreign countries and present Chinese drama, but he has only accepted the invitations of Japan, the United States, and Russia.

His tours to Japan in 1919 and 1924 resulted in the appearance of a number of "Mei-style" plays upon the Japanese stage. In 1930 he visited the United States and was most enthusiastically welcomed. He was elected to honorary membership in both the American Dramatic Association and the Organization of International Adventurers. He was the recipient of the honorary degree of Doctor of Letters from Pomona University and from the University of Southern California.

In 1934 he was invited by Soviet Russia to give performances in Moscow and Leningrad. The Chinese Government sponsored the trip, so in January, 1935, he began the journey in the boat sent by the Russian Government. Among the ovations he received, those for "The Valiant Fisherman and His Daughter" (see synopsis) were the greatest. Then while his troupe returned home, he toured Europe to investigate western drama. He has been repeatedly asked to bring his troupe to Europe, and he laconically replied, "I may, some day."

As a man he is shy, yet friendly; retiring, yet ambitious. He hates publicity, yet delights in society. He has been criticized for being too courteous and gentle, and for lacking at least one human characteristic, temper.

His boyhood schooling was desultory; his education has been attended to mostly by private tutors. Even up to the present time, in the midst of his manifold social obligations, he reserves at least three hours a day for study and research in the spirit of

"One who never turned his back, but marched breast forward."

PART I

—

Background

脩齡先生惠存

程硯秋敬贈

Illus. 3.   Ch'eng Yen-ts'iu

Illus. 4.   Ch'êng Yen-ts'iu in the Rôle of Liu Ying-ch'un
PLAY: *Liu Ying-ch'un or The Suspicious Slipper*

The Chinese Theatre

N the early days there was no permanent establishment like the theatre of today. On special occasions voluntary contributions were collected from the families of the neighbourhood to pay the actors. A temporary two-storied structure was erected, the ground floor being used for the dressing room and the first floor for the stage. The spectators seated themselves at their ease in the open air on stools or benches brought from their own homes, and arranged along the sides and in front of the stage.

There were also private performances, sponsored by rich families or officials, to entertain their guests or to celebrate certain occasions. These shows were usually given in the main hall of the host's stately mansion and therefore only the invited guests were admitted to this kind of performance. The honoured guest may order his favourite play to be performed—popularly known as "Tien-hsi."[1]

In the later dynasties, besides the permanent stage in the temples, "teahouses" began to be used for theatrical performances. People went

---

[1] "Tien-hsi" (點 戲), to order a play to be performed. If the Emperor, a noble or any special guest was in the audience, the man in charge of the theatrical group offered him the repertoire of plays and a pen with which the honoured guest "dotted" his favourite plays. These were immediately performed in the order designated, even if the play in progress were not yet finished. Hence, up to this day, the term "tien-hsi" (to dot a play) is used if one wants another to do a certain business for him.

there to sip tea while the performance was going on. That was why tables and stools (Illus. 6a, R) were put where we have our stall seats today. Originally, only tea was sold and the admission fee for the show was included in the "tea money." This custom, however, was changed and though an admission fee was charged for the show with tea money as its accessory, the theatre still retained the name of "teahouse." Tables were sold in entirety like boxes and individuals could only obtain inferior, cheaper seats on the sides of the stage or behind the tables (Illus. 6a, U). Later, "tien-hsi" began to develop in these "tea houses" and for each of the specially ordered plays an extra fee was charged.

The stage was almost square. A red or black lacquered pillar (Illus. 6a, o) at each front corner supported the projecting roof structure. Under the middle front of this roof and facing the audience, a large wooden board, lacquered or gilded, and bearing the name of the "teahouse," was hung. When a show was on, the stage was almost empty. At the back of the stage there usually hung a beautiful, embroidered curtain (Illus. 5, 6a, N) in which there were two openings, through which the actors made their entrance and exit. The entrance on the left (Illus. 6a, K) was called "Shang-ch'ang-mên" (上 場 門) and the exit on the right (Illus. 6a, L) was "Hsia-ch'ang-mên" (下 場 門). There were two smaller, but no less beautiful curtains hanging over these "doors." The place where the orchestra used to sit was called "Chiu Lung Kou" (九 龍 口 literally, the nine-dragon entrance, Illus. 6a, J). The name originated from a practice of Ming-huang (A.D. 712-756), an Emperor of the T'ang Dynasty who was so fond of music that whenever his favourite, Yang Kuei-fei, was dancing, he himself directed the orchestra. It is said that nine dragons, the symbol of the Emperor, were carved on the platform where he sat. Any actor appearing had to pass His Majesty before he reached the centre of the stage and to pay him respect he had to stand a moment before the nine-dragon platform to let him examine whether his appearance and movement were pleasing to the eye. Now, even though the orchestra does not always sit at this place, the name "Nine-dragon Entrance" still denotes the location on the stage, at which every actor of today on his first appearance, stands a minute to perform a "Turning" sleeve (see Part II, Ch I, 1) or some other movement to let the audience inspect and classify

Illus. 5. The Back Drop
(*Left to right*) 1—The Messenger. 2—Mu-lan. 3 and 4—Mu-lan's
Parents. 5—Mu-wei.

him as to his artistry. Behind к the actors usually stood when they were ready to appear or when they sang or spoke to represent persons approaching from a distance or some bystanders responding to the character on stage.

As the ground floor seats were for men only, the first floor boxes were reserved for women. They were partitioned by screens (Illus. 6b, s). In front of the box seats there was a broad railing, higher than an ordinary table, to be used when serving tea. Behind the boxes were the dress circle seats (Illus. 6b, т).

The palace theatre was like the "teahouse," above mentioned, in structure, but was more elaborately carved. It had only one floor for the audience, but there were two stages instead of one, the upper (Illus. 7b, н') and the lower (Illus. 7a, н). Whenever celestial beings were portrayed, the upper stage was used to represent their abode, while at the same time those who took human rôles were acting on the lower stage. In one palace theatre there was a three-storied stage, the bottom being used to represent the realm of devils or spirits of the dead. The seats opposite the stage (Illus. 7a, s′) were allotted to the Emperor and his royal family while those on the sides (Illus. 7a, R′) were for officials and court ladies. The different sexes were never permitted to sit together.

With the influx of western architecture, the modern Chinese theatre has done away with the pillars on the stage, the lacquered board, etc. Customs, too, have changed, the most important of which being women's preference for the more expensive stall seats rather than the boxes where ladies were formerly compelled to sit.

The back embroidered drop with the entrance and exit openings remains the same, but two additional doors, further to the sides and more to the front (Illus. 8a, K′ and L′), are being used for entrance and exit. Much to the disgust of the lover of old Chinese drama, realistic scenery is sometimes used on the stage (Illus. 9). In short, the Chinese theatre of today has been very much modernized.

KEY TO ILLUSTRATIONS No. 6A—No. 8C.

A	Street Entrance	O	Pillar
A′	Royal Entrance	P	Dressing Room
B	Entrance	Q	Stage Entrance
B′	Officials' (or Court Ladies') Entrance	Q′	Upper Stage Entrance
C	Ticket Office	R	Reserved Seats
D	Lobby	R′	Officials' (or Court Ladies') Seats
E	Bar Room	S	Boxes
F	Lounge	S′	Royal Box
G	Stalls	T	Dress Circle Seats
H	Stage	U	Seats
H′	Upper Stage	V	Stairs
I	Set	W	Gentlemen's Lavatory
J	Orchestra	X	Ladies' Lavatory
K,K′	Shang-ch'ang-mên (Entrance)	Y	Scenic Properties
L,L′	Hsia-ch'ang-mên (Exit)	Z	Exit
M	Off Stage	a	Business Office
N	Back Drop	b	Cloak Room

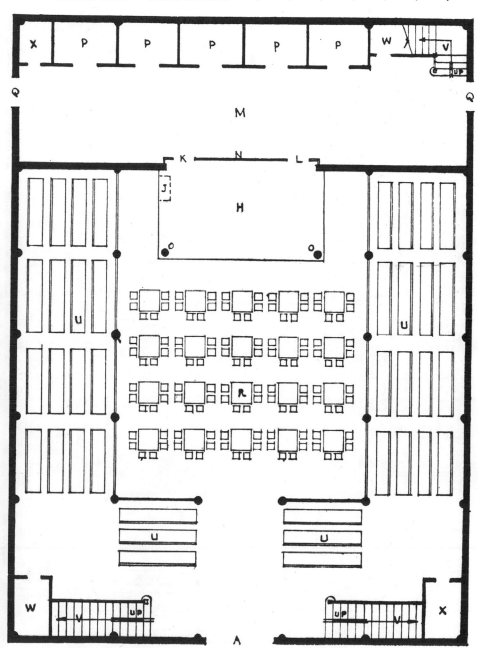

Illus. 6a. The Ground Floor Plan of an old-fashioned "Teahouse"

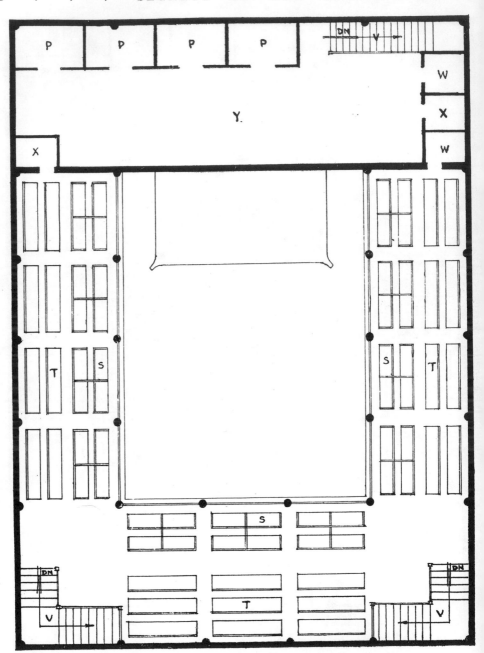

Illus. 6b. The First Floor Plan of an old-fashioned "Teahouse,"

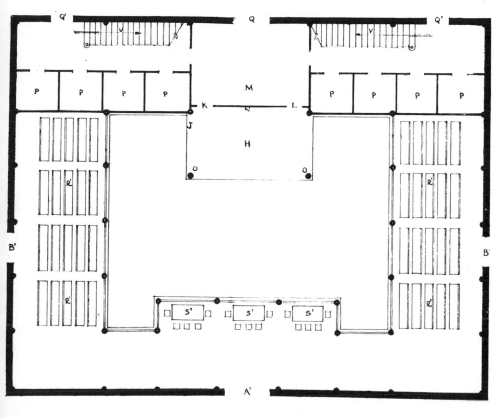

Illus. 7a. The Ground Floor Plan of a Palace Theatre

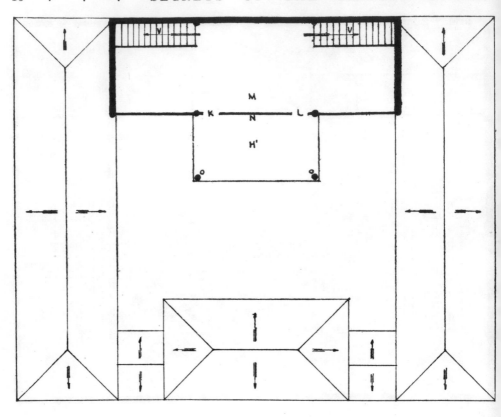

Illus. 7b.   The First Floor Plan of a Palace Theatre

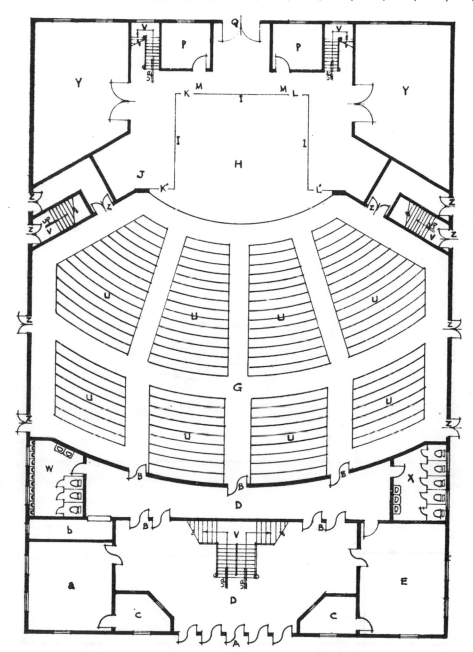

Illus. 8a. The Ground Floor Plan of a Modern Theatre

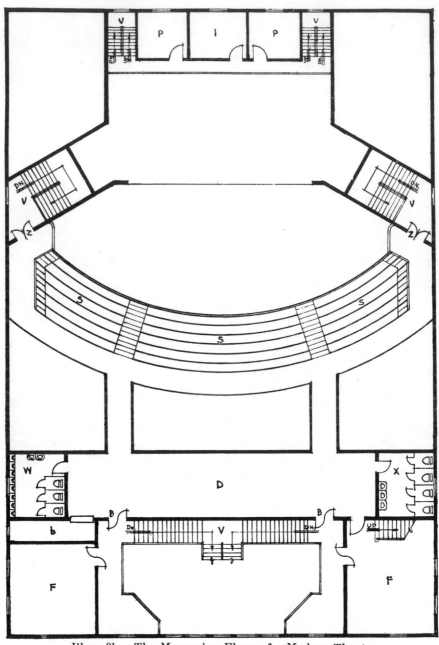

Illus. 8b.   The Mezzanine Floor of a Modern Theatre

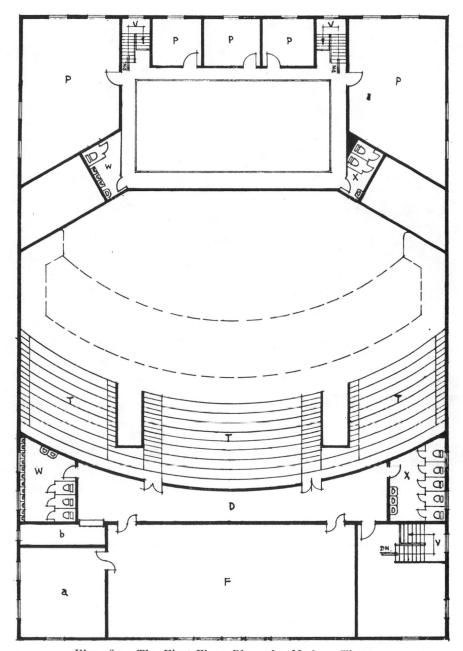

Illus. 8c. The First Floor Plan of a Modern Theatre

Illus. 9.   A Stage with Scenery

(*Left to right:*   The Maids, by Yao Yü-fu, Mei Lan-fang and Wei Lien-fang;
The Master, by Chiang Miao-hsiang).

Illus. 10.   "Tou-p'ung" ("Tan" by Mei Lan-fang); "K'ai-k'ao"
("Wu-ch'in" by Kin Shau-shan)

PLAY: *The Final Parting between the King and His Favourite.*

Illus. 11. "Tieh-tzŭ"; The Attention Sleeve (by Mei Lan-fang)

The Costumes and Stage Properties

In the very early days, actors, as well as stage properties, were owned by the rich. Special servants were appointed to control them. Naturally the drama was very simple and was produced on a small scale, but, as time passed, additions and alterations to the ancient plays made the art more and more complicated. In the T'ang Dynasty (A.D. 618-907) the Emperors became interested and began to patronize the art, so the costumes and stage properties were much better than before. Moreover, in the late Ch'ing Dynasty (A.D. 1644-1911) the rich, extravagant salt merchants offered specially woven silk to the Emperor to be made into elaborate costumes. The actors who played gods and goddesses wore the most beautiful robes. The stage was so spectacular that millionaires began to patronize it and the paraphernalia became so complicated that professional property-men had to be hired to take charge of the innumerable kinds of theatrical property. Now its scope has been further broadened by Mei Lan-fang's introduction of "ku-ch'uang" (古 裝 literally, the ancient apparel, Illus. 9, 37, 69, 80). He follows the fashion in women's dress of more than two thousand years ago.

There are strict conventions that the colour and style of costume must correspond with the status of the person, the character he represents and the occasion when he appears, *e.g.*

17

Illus. 12. "Mang" and "Yü-tai" (by Mei Lan-fang)

The Emperor	yellow
The members of the royal household	light yellow
The honourable or respectable class	red
The virtuous and kind	blue
The young	white
The old	brown
The straightforward and brusque	black

At formal, state occasions:

Both civil and military officials wear "mang" (see below).

On ordinary days, when off duty:

The characters wear "Tieh-tzŭ" (see below).

On the battlefield or when reviewing troops:

The military officials wear "K'ai-k'ao" (see p. 21).

The actors of today, however, enjoy much freedom in choosing their costumes. So long as they suit the taste of their audience, they are allowed to discard some of the old conventions.

The following are some important kinds of costumes:

1. MANG (蟒), the official robe (Illus. 40). This robe has a round collar, and long "rippling-water sleeves" (see p. 77). It is embroidered with dragon designs and at the lower edge with water-waves. It is usually made of satin and is worn on state occasions or at other formal celebrations. Robes for the female characters are shorter (Illus. 12, 40).

2. YU-TAI (玉帶), the precious-stone belt (Illus. 12, 40). This belt is made of some hard material inlaid with pieces of semi-precious or imitation stones. It is always worn with the "mang" a little below the waist.

3. TIEH-TZU (褶子), the everyday apparel (Illus. 11). It also has long "rippling-water sleeves" and is buttoned only at the collar and the waist. It may be made of stiff satin or soft crepe, either embroidered or plain, in black or in bright colours. The plain black kind is worn oftener than the "Tieh-tzŭ" in other colours. The white sash may or may not be used. "Tieh-tzŭ" worn by the male character is much longer. The front piece overlaps towards the right side, therefore it is buttoned under the arm (Illus. 43).

Illus. 13.   "P'ei" and "Ch'un" with Embroidered Panels (by Ch'êng Yen-ts'iu)

4. P'EI (帔), the overcoat (Illus. 13, 33). Unlike "tieh-tzŭ" it is buttoned only at the waist for the collar is very low and the whole dress reaches to the knees. It may cover the "tieh-tzŭ." It may be plain or embroidered with birds, flowers, dragon, phoenix or any other design. It is to be worn as a party dress on less formal occasions than when the "mang" is used.

5. CH'UN (裙), the skirt (Illus. 11, 13, 33). Skirts are worn by female characters only. They may have plain or embroidered front and back panels, the side-pieces being usually plaited. The formal official skirt is made of red satin, always with embroidered panels. When a skirt (or an additional skirt) is fastened about the bust, it represents a poor, wretched or distressed woman or maiden (Illus. 36). Sometimes it symbolizes travelling on a long journey for it shows that the character is not properly clad.

6. K'U-AO (袴 襖), the blouse and trousers (Illus. 62, 63), or CH'UN-AO (裙 襖), the blouse and skirt (Illus. 18). A "hua-tan" (see p. 37) usually wears a short blouse with short sleeves and trousers, or sometimes a skirt instead of the trousers. All of the costumes are in brilliant colours and embroidered in beautiful designs. An embroidered sash is always worn by a "hua-tan."

7. K'AN-CHIEN (坎 肩), the sleeveless jacket (Illus. 18, 44). This is commonly worn by soubrettes. There are two kinds, one reaching to the knees (Illus. 44) and the other, to the waist (Illus. 18, 63, 84). It may be plain or embroidered with beautiful designs in bright colours.

8. TOU-P'UNG (斗篷), the cape (Illus. 10, 21). The cape is worn by both male and female characters while travelling, or just after leaving the bed to show that the character has not finished dressing. Sometimes it is worn to represent illness or being outdoors late at night. It is very long, reaching almost to the feet, and may be plain or embroidered. Sometimes it has a heavy fringe along the lower border.

9. K'AI-K'AO (鎧 靠) the armour (Illus. 10, 23, 56, 57, 87). Characters of military type wear this costume on state occasions or on the battlefield. It is usually made of satin, embroidered and with tight sleeves. The lower part of the dress consists of four panels with an embroidered dragon or tiger head on the front panel at the waist. A mirror called "the heart-protecting glass" is often worn on the breast (Illus. 21, 54, 59).

The armour for the female rôles has numerous vari-coloured, embroidered streamers hanging, skirt length, with the panels comparatively shorter than those on the male warrior's costume. Sometimes tiny bells are fastened on the ends of these streamers.

10. K'AO-C'HI (靠旗), the military flags (Illus. 23, 56, 57, 87). Four flags, embroidered with dragon, phoenix or flower design, triangular in shape and of the same colour as the armour, are worn on the back of the generals. They got their origin from the idea that generals needed to give orders on the battlefield. The flag was to be used to prove the authenticity of the order.

11. SENG-I (僧 衣), the monk's (or nun's) attire. A monk (or a nun) wears a cap and a gray or yellow coat, sometimes with a long, sleeveless jacket over it. There is, however, another class of nun, who wear their hair just like ordinary women. On the stage they are allowed to wear the bright-coloured "tieh-tzŭ" but over it there must be a long sleeveless jacket embroidered in rhomboid designs. The headdress

和
尚
巾

The Cap

僧
背
心

The Jacket

with tassels and two embroidered streamers is peculiarly long at the back. A duster is always held by these religious characters (Illus 14).

12. FU-KUEI-I (富 貴 衣), the beggar's costume (Illus. 66). To represent a beggar or a wretched person, the actor wears a "tieh-tzŭ" patched with irregular-shaped pieces of silk or cloth in different colours. If he wears a cap or hat, it is similarly patched. It is called "the dress of the rich and the noble," meaning that the wearer someday may become better off financially and socially.

13. CH'I-CH'UANG (旗 裝), the Mandarin style of dress. From head-gear to shoes this style worn by the Manchus is different from the above-mentioned costumes. For instance, the shoe has a 2½ by 3-inch wooden block nailed to the centre of the sole (Illus. 91). Therefore, unless accustomed to this kind of shoe, the wearer finds walking rather difficult. The coat is very long, plain or embroidered, but never with

"rippling-water sleeves." Sometimes a short sleeveless jacket is added to an everyday coat, the front of which overlaps towards the right side, (Illus. 15). The official coat opens and is buttoned down the centre front. It is always made of satin (Illus. 27).

Besides the dress, the art of decorating the head and face of the female impersonator began to develop. Formerly, the "tan" (see p. 37) used only a piece of blue gauze as a headdress. Not much decoration was considered necessary, but this simple headdress did not match the elaborate costumes. Therefore, more beautifying touches had to be added to the head and face. Specially trained beauty artists became a necessity. Even the face-powdering, eyebrow-drawing, painting, hair-dressing, etc., were done by these professionals, and artistic forms of coiffure were invented. These decorative methods are still in vogue.

Stage properties were no less complicated than the above-mentioned details. Only a few examples have been selected for description:

山
石
片

A "Hill" or "Mountain"

1. SHAN (山), a hill or mountain.

   a. A chair lying on its side and placed behind a board painted with a mountain design stands for a hill or mountain.

   b. A chair may stand for a hill or mountain. The actor mounts the chair and steps down on the other side to show that he has crossed over a mountain.

令
箭
Lin-tsien

聖 旨
Sheng-chih

2. LIN-TSIEN (令箭), the mandate arrow. This arrow represents the command of some powerful man or woman that the bearer be allowed to pass freely any post or station, closed to ordinary persons.

3. SHENG-CHIH (聖旨), the royal mandate. A roll of yellow, embroidered silk, rectangular in shape when unrolled, bears the two words "sheng" and "chih" (literally, the royal mandate) and stands for the Emperor's order or proclamation. While the mandate is read it is held with the side bearing the words towards the audience.

馬鞭

Ma-pien

燈籠

Lantern "A"

燈籠

Lantern "B"

漿

Tsiang

4. MA-PIEN (馬 鞭), the horse-whip. A horse-whip stands for a horse and the actor holding it is supposed to be on horseback or leading a horse. When a whip is thrown on the stage, it means that the horse is let loose to graze or is fastened to a post or tree. The colour of the whip indicates the colour of the horse.

5. TENG-LUNG (燈 籠), the lantern. Besides the royal lantern (A), the ordinary kind (B) is merely a wooden frame, the lower part of which is wrapped in red silk and the upper larger part in green. Each of the lanterns has a long handle and is carried about to represent night.

6. TSIANG (漿), the oar. The actor holding an oar in his hand represents a character on board ship.

帥旗

Shuai-ch'i

令旗

Lin-ch'i

車旗

Ch'eh-ch'i

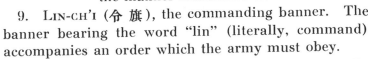

姓字旗

Sin-tzu-ch'i

7. SHUAI-CH'I (帥旗), the Commander-in-chief's banner. The banner bearing the word, "shuai" (literally, commander-in-chief), is often hoisted behind the character playing the commander-in-chief by his close attendant who must, of course, keep pace with his master.

8. SIN-TZU-CH'I (姓 字 旗), the personal banner. Sometimes a banner bearing the surname of the general is hoisted in the manner mentioned above.

9. LIN-CH'I (令 旗), the commanding banner. The banner bearing the word "lin" (literally, command) accompanies an order which the army must obey.

10. CH'EH-CH'I (車 旗), the wagon. Two flags, usually yellow, on each of which is drawn a wheel, represent a wagon. A servant carries the flags and the rider stands or walks between them. The flags are always brought on the stage by a servant whenever a wagon is needed and taken off as soon as the rider steps out.

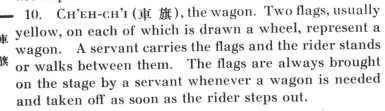

Shui-ch'i

Fung-ch'i

Pu-ch'êng 布 城

11. SHUI-CH'I (水 旗), the water banners. Banners with designs of waves and swimming fish represent water. Actors usually appear in fours each holding a water banner and constantly shaking it so as to make "waves." To represent suicide by drowning, the actor jumps towards them. Then they fold the flags around him and exit together.

12. FUNG-CH'I (風 旗), the wind banners. Black banners stand for windstorms. Actors, in fours, run across the stage to show the coming of a storm.

13. PU-CH'ENG (布 城), the city wall. A large rectangular piece of blue cloth, painted to represent the mortared bricks of a wall, stretched on bamboo poles and hoisted vertically, represents a city wall. There is an opening at the lower centre of the cloth so that the sides may be drawn back to represent the opening or closing of the city gates. Whenever a wall is called for, the property-men bring on stage this cloth wall. As the "gates" are not high enough for the actors to enter or leave the city easily, the wall is raised to facilitate their passage.

14. TENG TSO (燈 燭), light. A candle (Illus. 73) or table lamp not lighted is considered lighted. In recent years, however, some actors actually light the candle or lamp.

15. YIN (印), an official seal. A wooden block, about one-and-a-half inches square, wrapped in yellow silk or cloth represents an official seal. It is seen in the parallel plays, "The Suspicious Slipper" (汾 河 灣) and "The Meeting at Wu Chia Pu" (武 家 坡). There is another kind of official seal, similar in structure, only much larger.

16. CH'ENG-LOU (城 樓), the city-tower. To represent a person in a city-tower, the actor stands on a table placed behind the cloth wall. In "The Strategy of an Unguarded City," two tables are put side by side behind the cloth wall. On them is placed another table and a chair. The actor, playing Chu-kê Liang, first mounts the table and then sits behind the top table to play on the "ch'in" (琴 a seven-stringed musical instrument).

Illus. 14.   The Nun's Attire (by Mei Lan-fang)

PLAY: *A Nun Seeks Love*

17. Nui Ch'ang I (內 場 椅), the chair on the back-stage and Wai Ch'ang I (外 場 椅), the chair on the front stage. The former is the chair put behind the table in the centre of the back stage and the latter is the chair in front of the table.

18. Tao I (倒 椅), an overturned chair or a chair lying on its side. A chair not on its feet is no longer deemed a chair in the play, but something else, *e.g.* a mound, a common bench for the weary, etc.

19. Shou-chi (首 級), the decapitated head. A bundle about the size of a head wrapped in red cloth (sometimes with beard if an old man) indicates a decapitated head. Any character decapitated runs quickly off the stage and the property-man produces the head if called for.

20. Chang-tzu (帳 子), the bed, the tower, etc. An embroidered curtain, usually made of satin, represents a bed (Illus. 73) or a tower. Sometimes it is also used when high officials, civil or military, sit in session.

Illus. 15. A Manchu Lady in Everyday Attire (by Wang You Chun)

Illus. 16. "Lao-tan" (by Lee Too-ku'ei).

Illus. 17. "Chin-i" (by the Author)

CHAPTER THREE

The Musical Instruments

The orchestra for Chinese drama is named "Ch'ang-mien" (場面), literally "the face of the show." As limited space does not allow the description of all the musical instruments, only the following have been chosen:

號
筒

Hao-t'ung

嗩
吶

So-na

1-2. HAO-T'UNG (號筒) and So-NA (嗩吶), the horns. They are of the trumpet type and produce loud sounds. They are never played when a "tan" (see p. 37) is singing.

胡
琴

Hu-ch'in

3. HU-CH'IN (胡琴), the Chinese violin. This two-stringed instrument, played with a bow, is made of bamboo. It was introduced into China from the northern barbarian tribe Hu; hence, its name, hu-ch'in, meaning the violin of Hu. It is the leading instrument of the "p'i-huang" style (see p. 64). Its tunes are very high-pitched.

二
胡

Êrh-hu

4. ÊRH-HU (二胡), the "minor" Chinese violin. It is usually played to assist the "hu-ch'in" and its structure is similar to that of the latter, only its pitch is lower and its sound much softer.

31

Yüeh-ch'in

San-hsien

5-6. YUEH-CH'IN (月琴), the moon guitar, with four strings, and SAN-HSIEN (三絃), the three-stringed guitar. Both are used to assist the "hu-ch'in," therefore their tones are much softer than those of the "hu-ch'in."

7. PAN (板), the time beater. It is made of three pieces of hard wood, two of which are tied together, side by side, with the third piece hanging on a cord. The third piece is used to strike the other two. A clear sound is produced. The actor listens to it to keep time.

Pan

Huai-ku

Tan-p'i-ku

8-9. TAN-P'I-KU (單皮鼓), the one-sided drum and HUAI-KU (懷鼓), the breast drum. These two instruments assist the "pan" to indicate time in case the other instruments are so loud that the "pan" cannot be heard clearly.

10. T'ANG-KU (唐鼓), the large drum. It is seldom used in ordinary plays. When the more prominent actors sing the "fan-êrh-huang" tune[1] in the street scene in "Snow in June," this instrument is always used to assist the "pan." It is so delightful to the ear that it is now in vogue whenever that tune is sung. Moreover, in some of the dance scenes of Mei Lan-fang (梅蘭芳) and Ch'êng Yen-ts'iu (程硯秋), it is used to accompany the "hu-ch'in."

T'ang-ku

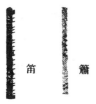

Ti and Siao

11-12. TI (笛) and SIAO (簫), the flutes. There are two kinds of flutes, "ti" (left) and "siao" (right). They look like the western flute, only the former when played is held parallel to the lips, with the second hole on the instrument—where a piece of bamboo tissue is pasted—serving as the mouth piece. In *K'un-ch'u* plays (see p. 63), "ti" is the leading instrument.

---

[1] "Fan-êrh-huang" is a tune relative to "êrh-huang" usually given in tragic plays.

笙

Shêng

星

Sin

鑼

Lo

小
鑼

Hsiao-lo

雲
鑼

Yuin-lo

鐃

Nao

P'i-p'a

琵
琶

13. SHENG (笙), the reed-organ. This instrument is made of a set of tube-like bamboos fastened together. Its notes are very soft and pleasing.

14. SIN (星), the cup-shaped bells. These bells help the "pan" to beat time. They are nearly always used with the large drum when the tragic songs in "fan-êrh-huang" are sung. They are made of brass in the shape of round cups, in the bottom of which a cord is fastened so that the outer end of it may be used as a handle. When one bell hits the other, a delightful sound is produced.

15-16. Lo (鑼), the gong and HSIAO-LO (小 鑼), the small gong. They are of the same structure, only the latter is much smaller. "Lo" produces very loud sounds and is generally used in playing the overture. Sometimes one or two strokes may be sounded between the musical passages or before some significant action takes place. The small gong is always used just before the "tan" steps on the stage.

17. YUIN-LO (雲 鑼), gongs in scale. This instrument consists of ten gongs, each being about two-and-a-half inches in diameter, hung in a wooden framework and each representing a different musical tone in the graduated series. A little wooden striker is used to hit the gongs.

鈸

Pa

18-19. NAO (鐃) and PA (鈸), the cymbals. They are very loud instruments made of brass, and generally used with the gong.

20. P'I-P'A (琵 琶), the lute. In olden times, "p'i-p'a" was the leading instrument in the orchestra of the Northern School of drama (see p. 62). It is made of wood and has four strings, a long neck and a bent head. Its sound box is semi-globular like that of the western ukelele.

FERNALD LIBRARY
COLBY-SAWYER COLLEGE
NEW LONDON, N.H. 03257

82587

As in the drama in other countries, the musical instruments are played to accompany the songs. Different, however, from practices in foreign shows, special musical passages, called "ku-mên" (過 門). literally "through the door," are played after each sentence, or line of poetry in songs, in which case the music is of a slow tempo, usually ¼ time. These musical passages give the actor time to rest or to make some artistic gestures, for the music must correspond with the actions, as well as with the atmosphere of the play. Therefore, a frequent theatre-goer can tell at once what kind of a song is going to be sung or what kind of action will follow, as soon as he hears the "ku-mên."

Formerly, the "Ch'ang-mien" (orchestra) was provided by the troupe manager, so the music was always the same, but after the leading stars began to write and sing their own compositions, these common orchestras could no longer meet their needs. Special musicians had to be trained for each particular artist. Therefore, the orchestra of the more prominent actors is always provided by themselves. As to the less prominent actors they only have violinists of their own.

Illus. 18. "K'an-chien"; "Hua-tan" (by the Author).

Illus. 19. "Kuei-mèn-tan" (by the Author)

The Character Types

All the characters in the Chinese drama except "tan" play male rôles.   The following may give some idea of the division of the character types:

TAN (旦), the female rôles.

(a) lao-tan (老 旦)—a dignified old woman (Illus. 16).

(b) chin-i (青 衣)—a virtuous woman.   This name, "blue coat," was derived from the colour of the garment, formerly worn in this rôle.   Now the dress is black (Illus. 17).

(c) hua-tan (花 旦 flower-"tan")—a coquettish woman or vivacious soubrette (Illus. 18).

(d) kuei-mên-tan (閨 門 旦 in-the-chamber-"tan")—a young or unmarried woman (Illus. 19).

(e) tao-ma-tan (刀 馬 旦 sabre-steed-"tan")—the military type of woman (Illus. 21).

(f) ch'ou-tan (丑 旦)—comedienne.

SHEN (生 Illus. 26).

(a) lao-shên (老 生)—a dignified aged man (Illus. 20b, 43).

(b) hsiao-shên (小 生 young-"shên") a youth (Illus. 65).

1. shan-tzŭ-hsiao-shên (扇 子 小 生 fan-"hsiao-shên")—a young man who always holds a fan (Illus. 22).

    2. chih-vei-hsiao-shên (雉尾小生 pheasant-feather-"hsiao-shên")—a young man who wears pheasant feathers on his headgear (Illus. 55).

   (c) wa-wa-shên (娃娃生 child-"shên")—a child (Illus. 67).

Those of the military type are known as "wu-lao-shên" (武老生 Illus. 23) and "wu-shên" (武生 Illus. 24, 25) respectively.

CH'OU (丑)—a comedian.

   (a) wên-ch'ou (文丑)—a clown (Illus. 70, 88).

   (b) wu-ch'ou (武丑)—a comedian of the military type (Illus. 25). This rôle requires a slightly-powdered face usually with the design of a butterfly.

CH'IN (淨), the painted-face characters.

   (a) hai-teu (黑頭 black-head)—the black face type (Illus. "*j*" p. 41).

   (b) fun-lien (粉臉 powdered-face)—the white-powdered face type (Illus. 48).

   (c) the mixed-type—the type of characters with faces painted in colours other than black and white.

   (d) wu-ch'in (武淨 military-"ch'in")—painted-face characters of the military type (Illus. 10, 72, 87).

As the painted-face character type is not found in the western drama, it may interest the reader to know something of the development of this peculiar feature of the Chinese drama.

Though no definite date can be found for the beginning of face-painting on the Chinese stage, yet we are sure that it was not perfected before the Ming Dynasty (A.D. 1368-1644), because before then only the wicked characters, such as the "white powdered faces," Nos. 1, 2 and 3 (see p. 43), wore paint. The reason why it did not flourish during the Yuan Dynasty (A.D. 1277-1368) was that only "shên" and "tan," who never wore painted faces, took the leading parts. It did not seem worth while to develop the art of face-painting for the minor characters. Historians, however, have found that as far back as the Northern Chi Dynasty (A.D. 550-577) that Prince Lan-ling and later Ti Ts'ing of the Sung Dynasty (A.D. 960-1277) wore formidable masks on the battlefield to cover up their handsome faces in order to frighten their enemies.

During the Ming Dynasty, strict rules began to be set down as to which character should wear which face. As years passed, the facial make-up became more and more complicated. To show the gradual changes, the following painted faces which General Ma Wu wore have been selected:

明
朝
式

(*a*) The Ming Period
(A.D. 1368-1644)

乾
隆
時
代
式

(*b*) The Ch'ien-lung Period
(A.D. 1736-1796)

咸
豐
初
年
式

(*c*) The Hsien-fêng Period
(A.D. 1851-1862)

同
治
時
代
式

(*d*) The Tung-ch'ih Period
(A.D. 1862-1875)

光
緒
初
年
式

(*e*) The Kuang-sü Period
(A.D. 1875-1909)

From the fact that six terms for make-up are often spoken of among actors, in the order of main background, eyebrows, eye circles, nose, mouth corners and cheek lines, we can see how face-painting was developed. Special meanings are shown by the figures drawn on the faces, *e.g.*

(*f*) Cloud designs for the God of Clouds.

(*g*) Flame designs for the God of Fire.

(*h*) Leopard spots for a Leopard Devil.

(*i*) An elephant's face for the monster whose original form was an elephant.

黑
頭

墨
色

(*j*) A Moon [1] on the forehead of P'ao-tsen (包 拯), the wonderful judge, who could go to the Land of Spirits to find out the real facts from the dead.

(*k*) The double battle-axe design on the forehead of Tou Ėrh-tung (竇 二 東), the expert in fighting with that weapon.

Besides, actors use face-designs to show their respect or contempt for the ancient men whom they represent.

Different colours represent different characteristics.   At first, there were only five colours, indicating the following meanings:

    1.   Red—loyalty and uprightness.
    2.   Purple—same as (1) only less in degree; old age.
    3.   Black—simplicity and straightforwardness.
    4.   Blue—obstinacy and ferocity.
    5.   Yellow—hidden craftiness or cleverness.

Later, these colours were added:

    6. · Gold and silver—dignity (mostly gods and fairies).
    7.   Green—wickedness (ghosts and devils).
    8.   Pink and gray—old age.

As time passed, actors took much liberty in using the brighter colours with no other reason than to please themselves.

Generally speaking, there are the following nine kinds of painted-faces:

---

[1] The moon stands for night when the dead come forth and are active, whereas the sun stands for day, when the ghosts hide.

(a) The Predominant-colour Face
(整臉)

The whole face except
the eyebrows has only
one colour.

(b) The Trisected-tile Face
(三塊瓦臉)

The eyebrows are broadened and
lines are added above and below
the eyes so as to divide the forehead and the cheeks into three
parts.

(c) The Shattered Face (碎臉)

The face is painted with such
irregular designs and in so
many different colours that it
looks as if it had been broken.

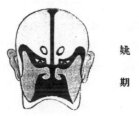

(d) The Aged Face (老臉)

The eyebrows are prolonged down
to the lower edge of the ears for it
was believed that the aged have
extremely long eyebrows.

(e) The Distorted Face (破臉)

The features of the face are
abnormal, e.g. an improperly
located eye or nose.

The predominant white colour represents a wicked and vicious man. In the following four kinds of faces, the degree of wickedness and craftiness is represented in direct proportion to the amount of white paint.

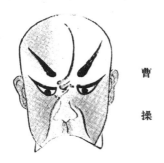

曹
操

(f) No. 1 "Ta-hua-lien" or the Entirely White Powdered Face (大白粉臉或大花臉).

殷
世
蕃

(g) No. 2 "Êrh-hua-lien" or the Half White Powdered Face (牛白粉臉或二花臉).

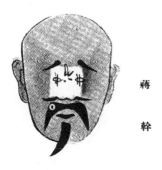

蔣

幹

(h) No. 3 "Hsiao-hua-lien" or the Slightly White Powdered Face (小白 粉臉或小花臉).

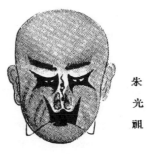

朱
光
祖

(i) The White-Nose Face (小尖粉臉或武丑)

Only the nose is painted white, but on the present stage the painted part is much bigger than it was before. It is usually worn by military comedians, whose character, though not dignified, is quite upright.

Besides, each character type has its own peculiar way of being acted, for instance, a "tan's" smile is not in the least like that of the other character types. A "ch'in" laughs robustly and loudly; a "lao-shên" laughs sturdily and in a dignified manner; a "ch'ou" enjoys much freedom which is denied other actors, while a "tan" must smile charmingly and with more tranquillity.

As to laughing and smiling, there are the following twenty kinds:

1. To laugh happily (正 笑).
2. To laugh coldly (冷 笑).
3. To laugh conceitedly (驕 笑).
4. To laugh jealously (妬 笑).
5. To pretend to laugh (假 笑).
6. To laugh surprisedly (驚 笑).
7. To laugh hysterically (傻 笑).
8. To laugh coquettishly (媚 笑).
9. To laugh coyly (羞 笑).
10. To laugh broken-heartedly (哭 笑).
11. To laugh scornfully (譏 笑).
12. To laugh insanely (瘋 笑).
13. To laugh treacherously (奸 笑)—often performed by actors playing successful wicked rôles.
14. To laugh heartily (大 笑)—the performer usually laughs aloud three times to show exceeding joy.
15. To laugh reluctantly (強 笑)—being dissatisfied at heart, yet feeling it impossible to do anything but laugh.
16. To laugh grievingly (氣 笑)—full of grief, yet without any means of expressing the feeling.
17. To laugh violently (狂 笑)—the actor usually laughs three times with upheld hands, either empty or with objects.
18. To laugh uneasily (僵 笑)—to hide embarrassment.
19. To laugh affrightedly (懼 笑)—though already out of danger, the person is still overwhelmed with the recollection of his past experience.
20. To laugh flatteringly (諂 笑)—commonly performed by the "slightly white powdered face" character.

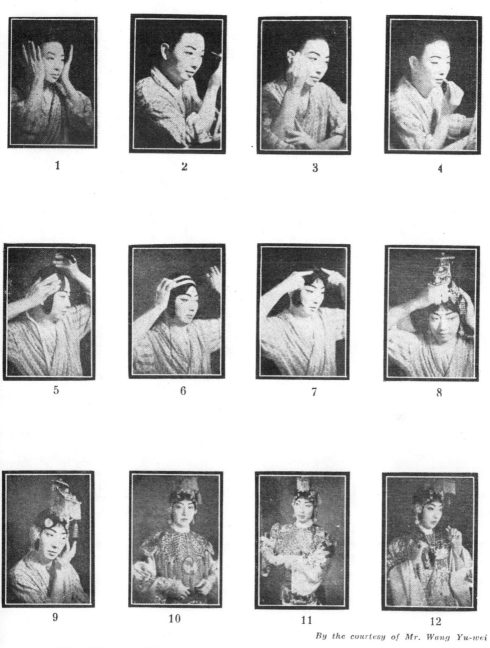

By the courtesy of Mr. Wang Yu-wei

Illus. 20a.   In The Dressing Room: "Tan"   (by Mei Lan-fang)

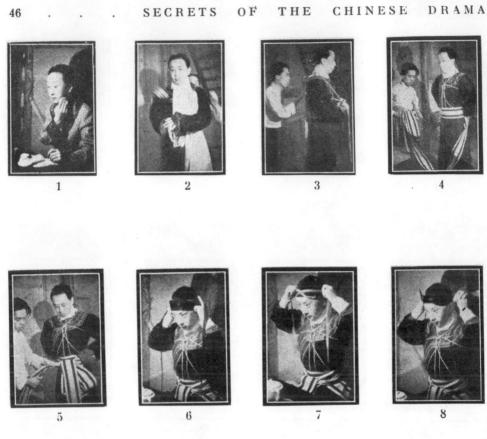

By the courtesy of Mr. Wang Yu-wei

Illus. 20b.   In The Dressing Room: "Lao-shèn" (by Ma Lien-liang)

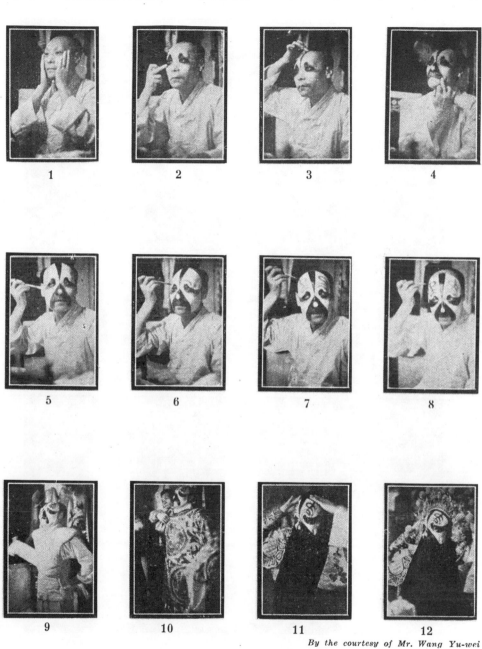

By the courtesy of Mr. Wang Yu-wei

Illus. 20c. In The Dressing Room: "Ch'in" (by Kin Shau-shan)

Illus. 21. "Tou-p'ung"; "Tao-ma-tan" (by the Author)

Illus. 22. "Shan-tzŭ-hsiao-shên" (by Ch'êng Yen-ts'iu, pláying that rôle in jest)

NOTE:—*Sometimes actors play rôles other than their professional ones, to amuse the audience.*

Illus. 23. "Wu-lao-shên"; "K'ai-k'ao" and "K'ao-ch'i"
(by Yu Shu-yen, China's leading "Lao-shên")

Illus. 24.   "Wu-shên"   (by Lee Wan-ch'un)

Illus. 25. (*Left*) "Wu-ch'ou" (by Wang Ch'ang-lin); (*Right*) "Wu-shên"
(by Ma Lien-liang)

SOME MALE ROLES

(For Illustrations see pp. 55-58.)

1. MA LIEN-LIANG in civilian dress.

Ma Lien-liang in the rôle of:

2. SIEH P'ING-KUEI. Play: The Red-maned Steed, Part II (三擊掌)*†
3. CHU-KE LIANG. Play: The Three Respectful Visits (三顧茅廬)
4. LIU P'ANG, THE KING OF HAN. Play: The Final Parting between the King and His Favourite (霸王別姬)*†
5. THE EMPEROR, SIEH P'ING-KUEI. Play: The Red-maned Steed, Part XI (迴龍閣)*
6. A HERMIT, CHIEH TSU-T'SIA. Play: Conflagration of the Mien Hill (焚綿山)
7. A WARRIOR, HSU TA. Play: Kuang-tai Chuang (廣太莊)
8. YAO-LI. Play: The Assassination of Ch'ing-chi (刺慶忌)
9. LIU PEI. Play: The Gallant Peace-maker (轅門射戟)*†
10. CHANG, THE TAOIST MAGICIAN. Play: A Tale of Three Dwarfs (五花洞)*†
11. FAN CHUNG-YU. Play: The Court Banquet (瓊林宴)
12. TENG CHIH. Play: Conquest along Five Lines (安居平五路)
13. SUN PE-YANG. Play: The Forged Mandate (假金牌)
14. LIU PEI. Play: Hero Judges Hero (煮酒論英雄)
15. CHI SIN. Play: The Conquest of Yung-yang (取滎陽)
16. CHAO K'UANG-NI, THE USURPER. Play: The Empress' Wrath (罵殿)*†
17. EMPEROR TSEN-TE. Play: The Emperor Steps Out (遊龍戲鳳)
18. THE FEARLESS MINISTER, CH'U SUI-LIANG. Play: The Ten Proposals (十道本)
19. PE HUAI. Play: The Able Public Clerk (失印救火)
20. CHU-KE LIANG. Play: The Strategy of an Unguarded City (空城計)*
21. T'SIN CH'IUNG. Play: The Invasion of Têngchow (打登州)
22. ME CHENG. Play: Hsüeh-yen, the Faithful Concubine (一捧雪)*
23. TIEN TAN. Play: The Charge of the Ox Brigade (火牛陣)

---

* See Synopsis.

† Ma Lien-liang has never taken these rôles in the respective plays. The pictures have been taken merely to show how the characters would look on stage.

24. YANG YEN-HUI. Play: Yang Yen-hui Visits His Mother (四郎探母)*
25. CHU-KE LIANG. Play: Offering at the River Loo (祭瀘江)
26. MENG YU-HUA'S FATHER. Play: The Royal Monument Pavilion (御碑亭)*†
27. MU-LAN'S FATHER. Play: Mu-lan, the Disguised Warrior Maiden (木蘭從軍)*†
28. THE PATRIOTIC AMBASSADOR, SU WU. Play: The Ambassador Shepherd (蘇武牧羊)
29. KUNG-SUN TSAN. Play: The Battle of the River P'an (盤河戰)
30. SIAO ENG. Play: The Valiant Fisherman and His Daughter (打漁殺家)*
31. LIU PEI. Play: The Fatal Camping Place (連營寨)
32. SIEH PAO. Play: A Family of Four Virtues (三娘教子)*
33. CHIAO HSUAN. Play: The Intriguers Intrigued (甘露寺)*
34. CH'U PIAU. Play: The Arrest of Fei Tê-kung (蚍蜡廟)
35. THE OLD GENERAL, YANG CHI-YEH. Play: The Death of Yang Chi-yeh (托兆碰碑)
36. SUNG SHIH-CHI, THE LAWYER. Play: Faithfulness, Fidelity, Purity, and Righteousness (四進士)*
37. WU SHEH. Play: The Pass of Chao, No. I (文昭關)*
38. WU YUIN. Play: The Pass of Chao, No. II (武昭關)*
39. WANG MANG. Play: Yuin T'ai Kuan (雲台觀)
40. SHENG YING. Play: The Lily Lake (蓮花湖)
41. WANG MANG. Play: Pê Mang T'ai (白蟒台)
42. THE RICH WIDOWER, HAN. Play: The Reward of Kindness (硃砂痣)*
43. WU TZU-SU. Play: The Pass of Chao, No. I (文昭關)*
44. K'UANG HUNG. Play: Loyalty Finds a Way (宇宙鋒)*†
45. TS'AI YUNG'S FATHER. Play: The Tale of the Lute (琵琶記)*†
46. THE CHIEF EXAMINER. Play: The Royal Monument Pavilion (御碑亭)*†
47. KUNG-SUN. Play: The Cost of Saving the Master's Son (八義圖)*†
48. GENERAL YANG PE. Play: The Two Faithful Officials (二進宮)

---

* See Synopsis.

† Ma Lien-liang has never taken these rôles in the respective plays. The pictures have been taken merely to show how the characters would look on stage.

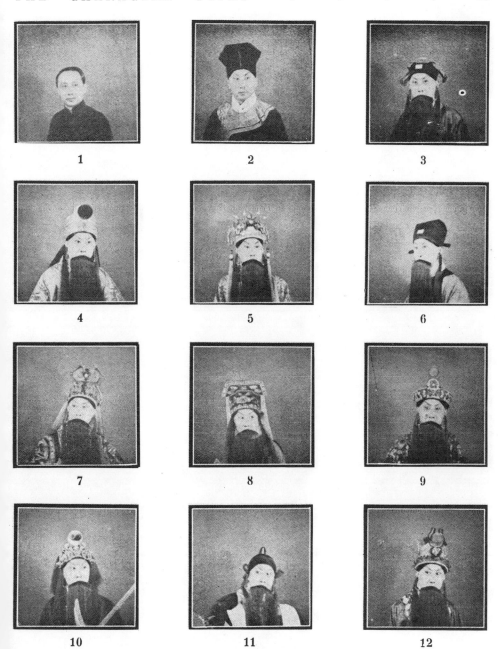

Illus. 26.   Some Male Rôles

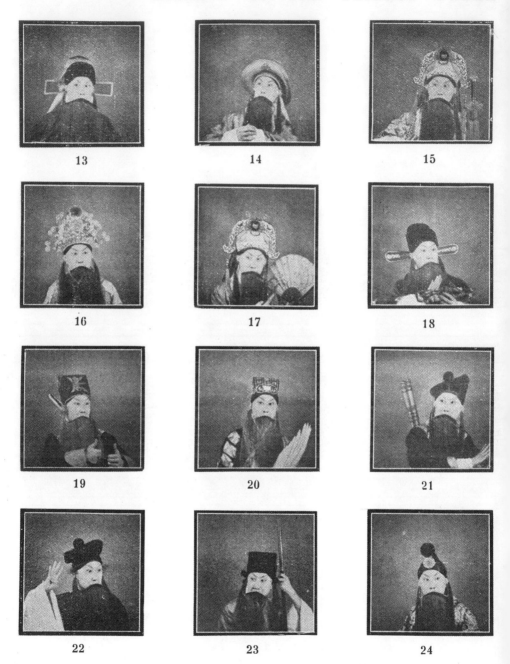

Illus. 26. Some Male Rôles

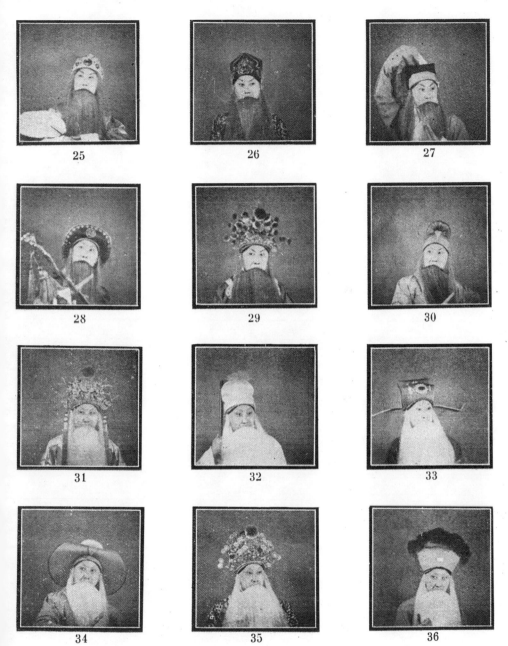

Illus. 26.   Some Male Rôles

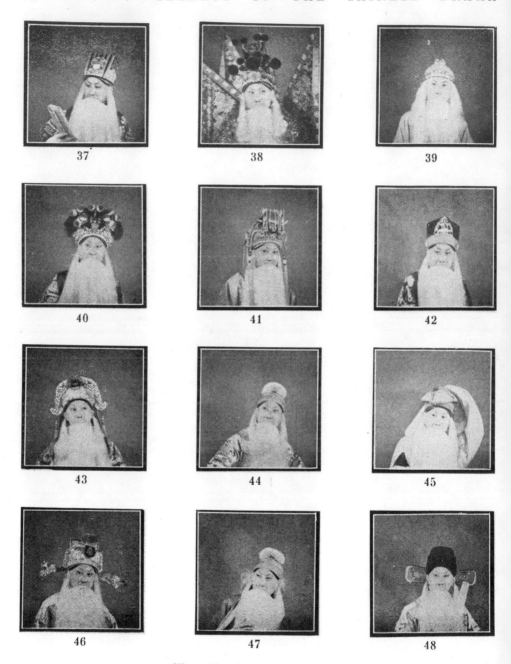

Illus. 26.   Some Male Rôles

The Development of the Chinese Drama

Gestures which are an essential part of the Chinese drama were derived from the ancient dance, but not until the T'ang Dynasty (A.D. 618-907) did the art of acting acquire its concrete form.   Some scenes in Mei Lan-fang's play, "Yang Kuei-fei," Part III, may give us an idea of how the T'ang Emperor, Ming Huang (A.D. 712-756), himself a musician, encouraged the dramatic art.

When it was felt that mere "p'ê" (白 dialogue) was insufficient to arouse the interest of the audience, songs were introduced; later, when even the addition of songs no longer satisfied the audience, the dance was developed.   This was not bringing in an unrelated art, for the actors themselves were conscious that when they concentrated their minds in singing, they involuntarily moved their hands and feet in accompaniment.   Therefore, in a short time the interpretative dance reigned in the dramatic world.

Great changes, however, intervened, and the dances were gradually transformed into the present conventional movements or gestures.   By studying carefully the dances of the T'ang Dynasty and by reading the names of the particular postures, one cannot fail to find a distinct analogy between the movements or actions on the present stage and those of the ancient dances, even though only a fractional part of the record has been preserved.   Besides, though not a few changes were made during the later dynasties, the fundamental principles remain

59

almost the same as in the early days, *e.g.* practically all arm and hand movements are still done in curves rather than in straight lines. Such gestures were (and still are) so appreciated by society that those performers who could only master singing were no longer as popular as those who could also dance.

Therefore, it is not exaggerating to say that the dance is the source of Chinese drama. The earliest form of dancing was the very simple kind given at the social gatherings of the primitive tribesmen or before the altars where offerings were made to the deities. At a later period, dances were performed only by picked men and women. Finally, professional dancers began to appear. The main purpose was to provide entertainment for the Emperor, for the nobility, and to please the gods. Those plays given at the temples were open to the masses and were of a more popular nature.

Even in the Chow Dynasty (1122-314 B.C.) the dance, though crude, was indispensable in the primitive plays. Those presented in the Han Dynasty (206 B.C.—A.D. 220) were also very simple and crude. Most of them depicted impossible stories of monsters or unusual happenings.

The far-reaching military conquests of the T'ang Emperors caused an influx of foreign music. The dramatic art was so encouraged by these rulers that it has been said drama reached its climax then. Satirical dialogue, lacking before that time, began to flourish in the T'ang plays.

Starting with the Sung Dynasty (A.D. 960-1277) simple comedies became very popular. Whole stories began to be portrayed. Even after Northern China was overrun by the barbarian tribes, Chinese civilization, including drama, was accepted as a whole by the invaders, and dramatic art remained almost unchanged.

Up to the Yuan Dynasty (A.D. 1277-1368) "shên," the male character, took the leading part in all of the plays. Not until this period was "tan," the female rôle, elevated to share the leading parts. Practically all the parts were sung in solo, though action and declamation were no less essential than singing in the play as a whole.

It was in this dynasty that the drama began to be popularly divided into two classes, namely, the Northern or "Tsa-chü" (雜 劇) and the Southern or "Hsi-wên" (戲 文). The following are the salient differences between the two types:

1. DIFFERENCES IN NATURE.

(a) *The composition of the play.* Each of the Northern Yuan plays was generally divided into four "turns" (折) in each of which a "shên" or a "tan" took the leading part. Only the actor who played that part sang, the other minor characters responded in speech. Whenever both "shên" and "tan" were equally prominent in a "turn" they sang alternately. Moreover, the leading part was not limited to the same character throughout the play, *e.g.* a "shên" or "tan" might play character A in the first "turn" and characters B and C in the following "turns." Thus he played the leading parts in all the "turns" but not the same character. As to declamation the usual order was (1) some passage of poetry, (2) the past life history of the character or self-introduction, and lastly, (3) the dialogue. The minor characters usually appeared on the stage first, gave some declamation or action and then followed the leading character, who also declaimed before he began to sing.

The Southern type was not limited to four "turns." A single play might contain from forty to fifty scenes, *e.g.* the representative play of this school, "The Tale of the Lute" (琵 琶 記), had forty-three scenes. Though they were much shorter than the Northern type scenes, the whole Southern play was at least six or seven times as long as "Tsa-chü." The parts were not sung in solo but in chorus or in turn by all or the majority of the characters, leading and minor.

Lines of poetry and self-introduction were similarly delivered as in "Tsa-chü," but sometimes, unlike the Northern play, the lines of poetry were divided among the characters and quoted in turn. Some more lines of poetry were recited at the end of the scene before the exit. Again in contrast to "Tsa-chü," almost every scene started with singing. Another dissimilarity was that the dance was much more popular in the Southern type than in the Northern plays.

(b) *The selection of songs.* In the Northern school, numbers of songs having the same keynote were arranged in a single set. All the lines in any set had the same rhyme and were sung in the standard Kai-feng (the former capital of the Sung Dynasty) dialect of Honan province.

The songs of the Southern type were not limited to the same keynote nor to one set for each play. On the contrary, there were several sets of songs in a single play.

(c) *The ending*. The Northern plays allowed tragic endings whereas the Southern type, though not without a very few exceptions, had only happy endings. Even the old tragic plays of the earlier dynasties were reconstructed for that purpose (see "Snow in June," Note II, p. 261).

2. DIFFERENCES IN MUSIC.

Though the two types were developed from the same origin, yet the intermingling of each type with the folk songs and local music rendered striking differences along the following lines:

(a) *Musical instruments*. In the South, the time beater, "pan" (see p. 32, Item 7), became the leading instrument. The flute was later added as an accompaniment, while in the North, the lute (see p. 33, Item 20) was the dominant instrument.

(b) *Singing method*. The Southern songs contained fewer words and were sung in prolonged tones, which ran continuously with the notes of the flute, for pause was not emphasized; but the Northern type had more words and tones were short. Pauses were strictly emphasized not only in sentences and words but even in the syllables of a single word. Therefore, the sweetness of the music of the Southern type was superior to that of the Northern, but its prolonged tones made the songs hard to understand and this difficulty was its chief defect.

(c) *Quality*. The Northern music was rigid, simple and stimulating while the Southern was flexible, elaborate and alluring.

In the early years of the Yuan Dynasty when the Tartars pushed southward, the northern "Tsa-chü" came with the conqueror. As it was a novelty to the southerners, it soon became very popular and supplanted the local "Hsi-wên." Before long, however, "The Tale of the Lute," the masterpiece of the latter type, began to attract great audiences and the "Hsi-wên" regained its former popularity, reaching its topmost position towards the decline of the Ming, the next, dynasty (A.D. 1368-1644).

After the northern "Tsa-chü" was accepted by the Ming people, each play was divided into five "turns." The songs were no longer limited to solos but were sung in duet and chorus as well as by turns in solo. In addition to the solo dance in the Yuan plays, dancing in groups was introduced.

During the reign of the Ming Emperor, Chia-Tsing (A.D. 1522-1567), the musical genius Wei Liang-fu (魏良輔), invented a new style of music and named it *K'un-ch'u* (崑曲), after his native place K'un-shan —a town near Shanghai. The plays of this Southern type, mostly romantic love stories, are the work of literary men, and are to be performed in a more exquisite and refined manner than the Northern kind. The songs are sung to the soft accompaniment of the flute.

Soon *K'un-ch'u* excelled the other older branches of the Southern school, such as the *Hai-yien* (海鹽), which originated in the district of Hai-yien, Chekiang province, and became prevalent in Taichow, Kasheng, Wuchow, Wenchow, etc.; and the *Yu-yao* (餘姚), which originated in Yu-yao and became popular in Yangchow, Hsuchow, Chinkiang, Changchow, etc. During the reign of the Ch'ing Emperors, Kang-Hsi (A.D. 1662-1723) and Ch'ien-Lung (A.D. 1736-1796), *K'un-ch'u*, having been introduced into the imperial palace, reached its climax. Returning after his visit to the South, Emperor Ch'ien-Lung brought back to the capital a whole troupe of *K'un-ch'u* actors, selected and presented by the rich and extravagant salt-merchants and local officials. Prior to this time the imperial theatrical department followed the Ming system by having the eunuchs perform on special occasions the seasonal plays for that particular day. Outsiders, however,—non-professionals—were sometimes summoned to assist the eunuchs.

Now, a new department, the "Literary Society" (雅部), presenting only *K'un-ch'u* plays, was set up parallel with the reorganized old theatrical system, newly named "Floral Society" (花部), and performed the following types of plays:

1. YI-YANG (弋陽腔). This type originated in Yi-yang district, Kiangsi province, and spread to Peking, Nanking, and the provinces of Hunan, Fukien and Kwangtung. Its origin can be traced to a period earlier than the reign of Emperor Van Lih (A.D. 1573-1620).

2. KAO (高腔). It has been said that when "Yi-yang" became popular in Peking, it was discarded in its native place; it found favour and flourished in Kao-yang district where it received the new name, "Kao." No stringed instruments, only drums, gongs, trumpets, etc., are used in this type, so the music is very loud.

3. CHING (京腔). During years of performance in Peking

"Yi-yang" was gradually altered into an almost entirely different form, constituting a separate school, popularly known as Ching.

4. P'ANG-TZU (梆 子 腔). The name was derived from the piece of bamboo called p'ang-tzŭ, which is employed by the director of the orchestra to beat time. Some important alterations gave a softening effect to the tune and made it very pleasing to the ear. While the original form was declining, this altered branch, now known as "Nan-p'ang-tzŭ" (南 梆 子·) was chosen by the "p'i-huang" school to accompany romantic songs in love scenes. Therefore it is entitled to share the present unsurpassed popularity of the latter school.

5. Ts'IN (秦 腔). This type, though reputed to have originated in Shensi province was in fact started in the province of Kansu. Its songs are never accompanied by the flute, but by "hu-ch'in" (the Chinese violin) assisted by "yüeh-ch'in" (the Moon guitar). Therefore, it is said that the essential constituent, "hsi-p'i" (西 皮) of the "p'i-huang" type, always accompanied by these two instruments, is but a synonym of Ts'in.

6. P'I-HUANG (皮 黄). It is known to be a combination of "hsi-p'i" and "êrh-huang" music. The name "êrh (literally, two) huang" is derived from the fact that it originated in the two Huang districts in Hupeh province, namely, Huang-kon, and Huang-pi. Its songs are accompanied by the high-pitched "hu-ch'in," which instrument was introduced into China from the northern tribe, Hu.

7. LUAN-TAN (亂 彈). This school consisting of all the other types except K'un-ch'u is called a "medley," because of the mixture. Some writers, however, hold that it has been so named because the orchestra of this school consists of many kinds of musical instruments.

8. LOCAL PLAYS. In many districts plays are given in the colloquial dialect, which is little known or appreciated outside of that locality. While these are of small dramatic value they do provide entertainment for the country people who have all too little to alleviate the monotony of their lives.

During the last years of Emperor Chia-chun (A.D. 1796-1821) when K'un-ch'u and Yi-yang were at their height, some experienced actor of Anhwei province selected the best points of those schools, added some of his own invention, mingled "hsi-p'i," "p'ang-tzŭ" and "êrh-huang" together and called this pot-pourri "p'i-huang." Since almost all the "p'i-huang" actors were Anhwei men, they called themselves the Anhwei Troupe (徽 班). The tunes were so artistically welded together that it became a powerful rival of the Literary Society. Some other geniuses like Ch'êng Chang-kêng (程 長 庚), an expert not only in "êrh-huang" but in *K'un-ch'u,* Yu San-shêng (余 三 勝), expert in "hsi-p'i," Wang Kuei-fung (汪 桂 芬) and Tan Hsin-pei (譚 鑫 培) cleverly improved the "p'i-huang" plays.

Before long, the different schools stood thus:

(*a*)   Literary Society (雅 部).................K'un-ch'u (崑 曲)

(*b*)   Floral Society or Lüan-tan (?) (花 部或亂 彈)

Yi-yang (Kiangsi) ————> Kao (Kao-yang) (高)
(弋 陽) Ching (Peking) (京)

P'ang-tzŭ ————————> Nan-p'ang-tzŭ (南 梆 子)
(梆 子)
Ts'in (Shensi)—Hsi-p'i
(秦)　　　　 (西 皮)
Erh-huang (Hupeh) ——> P'i-huang (Peking)
(二 黃)　　　　　 (皮 黃)

At the beginning of the reign of Emperor Tao-kuang (A.D. 1821-1851) *K'un-ch'u* began to give way to "p'i-huang" for these reasons: First, because the love stories of the *K'un-ch'u* type seemed to have been written after the same pattern and therefore were not so interesting as the various ethical "p'i-huang" plays; Second, the literary songs were not as easy to understand as the other simple kind. It is like the old saying, "The deeper the music, the less appreciative the audience." And finally, nearly all the *K'un-ch'u* actors were natives of Soochow, which city was, of course, their headquarters. When the Taiping Rebellion broke out, Soochow fell and suffered such great losses that *K'un-ch'u* has never been able to recover from the calamity.

About the year 1921, some rich families in Soochow contributed a considerable sum of money with which a *K'un-ch'u* Renaissance Institute was established to train young boys for this dramatic profession. Though not without significant results, it is far from being in a position to compete with its rival, the "p'i-huang" type, which is peerless in the dramatic realm.

During the decline of the Ch'ing Dynasty (A.D. 1644-1911), the influx of western drama caused the production of a group of modern plays in which realistic scenery was introduced. These plays were—and are— shunned by the conservatives for the latter strongly hold that as the stage is limited fundamentally in space and time, it cannot look or be real. There must be imagination! How could a high mountain be actually moved and put on the stage? How could a big forest be transplanted?

It is the main purpose of the Chinese drama that the actor should produce an artistic effect rather than be true to life. For it is the ideal, not the real, that is intended to be emphasized. The aim is to present the show as artistically as possible without heeding whether or not the details are true to life. Not only in intonation, such as musical cadence in speech, and rhythmical recitation in poetry, but also in bodily movements such as conventional gait and sleeve movement, there are striking differences from the sounds and actions of daily life. Various kinds of strict canons or rules must be carefully observed by the actors. Any expression of feeling—a smile, a frown, a sigh, an indication of surprise —must be conventionally given in accordance with special music. If an actor can make his audience feel and appreciate what he means to present in the play, it is sufficient. Therefore, the stage for purely Chinese plays is practically bare, having only a table and some chairs.

Since, until recent years, the great actors, Ch'êng Chang-kêng, Wang Kuei-fung, Tan Hsin-pei, and Sun Chu-sien (孫菊仙) played "lao-shên" (upright, aged masculine rôles), naturally persons playing this rôle occupied the foremost position. Then, the long-established ranking system was revolutionized by Mei Lan-fang after his successful visit to Shanghai in 1913. For the first time in China's histrionic record, a "chin-i" (rôle for good and dignified woman), began to be ranked above "lao-shên," the heretofore superior partner. Since 1917 when Dr. Mei was chosen "The King of Actors," "tan" has maintained the foremost position. After this rôle assumed leadership on the Chinese stage, the four most prominent female impersonators began to be talked of as "The Four Kin-kongs" (四大金剛 the four immense figures which sit or stand on the sides of the front hall in every Chinese temple of considerable size. The term is now used in the Chinese vocabulary to represent great persons or things). The "kin-kong tan" actors are:

Mei Lan-fang (梅 蘭 芳) . . . . (Frontispiece)
Ch'êng Yen-ts'iu (程 硯 秋) . . . (Illus. 4)
Shang Hsiao-yuin (尚 小 雲) . . . (Illus. 27)
Sün Hui-shên (荀 慧 生) . . . . (Illus. 28)

The four "kin-kong tan" actresses are:

Hsüeh Yen-ch'in (雪 艷 琴) . . . (Illus. 29)
Chang Ngê-yuin (章 遏 雲) . . . (Illus. 30)
Sin Yen-ts'iu (新 艷 秋) . . . . (Illus. 31)
Tu Lee-yuin (杜 麗 雲) . . . . (Illus. 32)

Though many high class people went on the stage as amateurs, yet the professional players as a class were despised. They were looked upon as belonging to almost the lowest caste, chiefly because not a few actors conducted themselves in a despicable manner. Not until ambitious, upright actors, such as Mei Lan-fang, Yu Shu-yen (余 叔 岩), Sun Chu-sien and Ch'êng Yen-ts'iu came into prominence, was the dramatic profession regarded as respectable by the conservative society of China. Another reason that the status of actors has been raised is that some of them have gifts other than dramatic, such as painting (see pp. xxii, xxiii) and writing (see pp. ix, xiv).

Illus. 27. The Mandarin Official Robe (by Shang Hsiao-yuin, in the Rôle
of the Empress Dowager).

PLAY: *Yang Yen-hui Visits His Mother*

Illus. 28.   Sün Hui-shên in the Rôle of Hè Yü-feng

Illus. 29.   Miss Hsüeh Yen-ch'in in the Rôle of the Empress
PLAY: *The Empress' Wrath*

Illus. 30.   Miss Chang Ngê-yuin in the Rôle of Mêng Yü-hua

PLAY: *The Royal Monument Pavilion*

Illus. 31. Miss Sin Yen-ts'iu in the Rôle of Yü-ching-tao-jên

PLAY: *Yü-ching-tao-jên*

Illus. 32.   A Posture on Horseback (by Miss Tu Lee-yuin)

PART II

Technique

DRAMATIC ACTIONS

In summarizing the dramatic actions, it may be said that they comprise the following six movements, namely: sleeve, hand, arm, foot, leg, and waist. In the following chapters, when only one hand, foot, arm, or leg is mentioned, unless otherwise stated, it does not mean that only one is used in performing that particular movement.

Sleeve Movements

Long sleeves were introduced in order to give more grace to the body movements. In the later dynasties, however, it was felt that these sleeves were too heavy for quick motions. Therefore, for the sake of lightness as well as cleanliness, cuffs, from one-and-a-half to two feet long and made of sheer silk, usually white in colour, were attached to the sleeves, and left open at the seam. This extension of the sleeve, when flourished, looked like flowing water, hence the term "Rippling-water sleeve" (水袖). Generally, the leading artists wear longer sleeves than the minor actors, not only because they are masters of sleeve technique, but because they can afford to own more expensive costumes.

From the saying, "the longer the sleeves, the better the dance," we can easily see why sleeve movements are the most important of all dramatic actions. In olden times, in the dance, which was the main feature of the drama then in vogue, long sleeves were almost indispensable. Consequently, sleeve movement was very carefully studied and taught, as grace was imperiously demanded of both male and female characters. Moreover, like stage walking, sleeve movements should be performed in accord with the rhythm of the music. Each of them indicates some definite meaning; for instance, a "turning" sleeve (see p. 79) is a signal call for music; a "repulsing" sleeve (see p. 81) an expression of disagreement, etc.

Illus. 33. The Concealing Sleeve (by Mei Lan-fang)

There are more than fifty different kinds of sleeve movements.   In order to avoid pedantry, only those movements which are more commonly used on the stage have been selected.   In the following chapters, "sleeve" (with small "s") denotes the "rippling-water sleeve"; "R Sleeve" (with capital "s") stands for the real sleeve, and "hands," unless otherwise stated, means the hand hidden by the sleeve.   As to the technique of performance, the descriptions in this book emphasize the "tan's" movements.

1.   THE TURNING SLEEVE (抖 袖).

This is the most important sleeve movement, performed by all the actors.

Start with right hand, palm inward, a little below the chest.   Move downward and towards the right in a curve.   On reaching the front of the slightly bent right knee, make a quick turn at the wrist, and throw the sleeve backward and a little to the right.   The eyes should follow the motion of the sleeve and the body should lean forward in harmony with the hand movement.

The left hand may go through the same movements, but in the opposite direction.   Sometimes both hands may make the same movement either alternately or together.   In the latter case, the movements are called respectively "alternative-turning" sleeves (兩 抖 袖) and "double-turning" sleeves (雙 抖 袖).

Meaning: (a)   It serves as a warning to the orchestral director[1] that the actor is ready for a change, *e.g.* to sing, to talk, or to proceed with some new gesture.

(b)   It also serves as a link between two movements. Usually, when an actor makes his appearance, he first walks to "Chiu Lung Kou" (see Part I, Ch. I), where he stops for just a moment to let the audience have a clear look at him and see what kind of character he is to play.   Here he often performs this sleeve movement before he proceeds.

---

[1] "Chiao-pan" (叫 板), or the signal to orchestra.   The actor usually prolongs the last word of his declamation as a warning to the orchestra to be ready that he is about to sing.   At the same time a "turning" sleeve is performed.

Illus. 34.　The Aside Sleeve　(by Wang Shau-t'ing and Mei Lan-fang)

PLAY:　*The Suspicious Slipper*

2. THE ASIDE SLEEVE (背 供 袖).

This is also a very important sleeve movement, because it is performed by all characters.

Raise the right hand to the right side, level with the cheeks. Let the sleeve hang down naturally from the fingers (Illus. 34, 85). Sometimes the actor walks a few steps to the side of the stage away from the other players.

The "aside" on the Chinese stage has much the same meaning that it has in the West. Gestures made or words spoken to oneself in the presence of other characters on stage are considered either secrets revealed to the audience only, or private thoughts given aloud (Illus. 70, 76).

Meaning: It denotes that the other characters on the stage can no longer see or hear what the actor, with the sleeve thus raised, is doing or saying. For instance, he may express his secret plan, or give warning to his accomplice, or do anything that is not to be understood by the other characters.

3. THE CONCEALING SLEEVE (遮 袖).

The sleeve is raised just as in (2) only higher and more to the front. It should be held sufficiently high to hide the actor's face. A semicircle is formed with the arm. Unlike (2) the actor should remain silent with eyes looking down (Illus. 33).

Meaning: (*a*) To show embarrassment.
(*b*) To prevent oneself from being discovered.

4. THE REPULSING SLEEVE (摔 袖).

(a) After a circular wrist movement, throw the sleeve abruptly towards the person disliked. At the same time cast an angry look at him, and then turn the head in the opposite direction to show that no further intercourse is desired.

(b) Raise the right hand relaxed. When it reaches the front of the chest, by a graceful wrist movement, turn the palm toward the left front, letting the sleeve hang naturally from the extended fingers.

Illus. 35. The Greeting Sleeves (by the Author)

Incline the body a little to the right, and shake the head in negation (Illus. 72).
Meaning: To express dislike, anger, or repulsion.

5. THE SENDING-AWAY SLEEVE (揮 袖).

In a curve movement raise the hand to the front, slightly below the face, palm inward. Then by a circular wrist movement throw the sleeve forcefully outward from the body, either once or three times, using both hands alternately. In the latter case the actor steps backward in harmony with the hand movements.
Meaning: To send away a person or thing.

6. THE GREETING SLEEVES (萬福袖).

Place the left hand below the chest on the right side of the waist, and put the right hand on it. At the same time, make a graceful bow (Illus. 35).
Meaning: To show respect to the person greeted.

7. THE DUSTING SLEEVE (撣 袖).

Raise the left hand a little above the head, with folded sleeve and arm upheld in a curve. Simultaneously, bend a little forward at the waist, slightly brush the seat with the right sleeve, first to the right, then to the left, and again to the right, as if to dust the chair of the honourable guest or superior. Similarly, but in opposite directions, use the left hand to dust the chair. Again dust with the right sleeve (Illus. 41). Sometimes the movements are preceded by a ceremonial offering of wine, as is shown in the play "Killing the Tiger General" (see synopsis). This custom remains in real life.

For instance, in an old fashioned wedding celebration, the seat of the mother-in-law is to be thus "dusted" by the bride, only she may use a large silk handkerchief if she does not wear long sleeves.
Meaning: To show utmost respect or honour to the person to be seated.

8. THE UPHELD SLEEVE (翻 袖).

(a) When only one hand is used, this movement is usually made by the right hand. In addressing a person, raise the hand up a little to the front and above the head by a quick circular movement at the

Illus. 36. The Wretched Woman: The Upheld Sleeve (by Mei Lan-fang)

wrist. Throw the sleeve upward and inward so as to fold and let it rest on the back of the hand. At the same time, bare the "open" (see p. 99) left hand, palm outward, and touch lightly the raised right hand, calling the name of the person addressed. Usually, this movement is followed by a "turning" sleeve (see p. 79).

(b) In lamentation the sleeve is thrown upward and outward instead of inward, and hangs from the extended fingers of the supine hand (Illus. 36, 58).

Sometimes both sleeves are raised. The most beautiful way of performing this is to first raise the left hand as high as the lower chest. Then pass the right hand between the chest and the left hand. Lift the arm up in a curve a little above the head and towards the front; fold the sleeve outward from the head. Raise the left hand similarly and poise it about four inches from the right. Both arms should be upheld in graceful curves and a little in front of the head so as to hide a part of the face. Simultaneously, slightly stamp the right foot to show deep grief. This movement is beautifully portrayed in the plays "The Suspicious Slipper" and "Killing the Tiger General."

Meaning: (*a*)   To address a person, in sight, in a picture, at a distance or deceased.

            (*b*)   To express deep sorrow or remorse.

            (*c*)   To warn the orchestral director that the actor is ready to sing or to declaim.

            (*d*)   To show desperation in undertaking some serious task or dangerous enterprise.

9. THE ADDRESSING SLEEVE (捧 袖).

The Addressing Sleeve

Raise the left hand a little below the chin. Fold the sleeve. Bare the "open" right hand; touch lightly the raised left sleeve and greet the person to be addressed. This is usually done to a person who is present, but sometimes this movement is performed in mentioning the name of some beloved or honoured person who is absent.

Illus. 37. Looking Backward with Running Sleeves
(Sleeve Dance by Mei Lan-fang)
PLAY: *Ma-ku Offering Birthday Greetings*

The only difference between (8a) and (9) lies in the position of the hands. In (9) they are held much lower than in the preceding movement.

Meaning: (*a*) To show respect to the person addressed or mentioned.

           (*b*) To seek attention from the person addressed.

10. THE RESOLUTION SLEEVE (投 袖).

The right hand, raised level with the right shoulder, is turned at the wrist in an inward and upward circle, and then brought straight down with the hand prone. Simultaneously, the head is shaken and the words "Yã-bah" (也 罷) are spoken, meaning "I have reached a decision!" or "It seems as if this is the only course for me to pursue!"

Meaning: To reach a decision, *e.g.* to determine to sacrifice one's life.

11. THE SHADING SLEEVE (蔭 袖).

Raise and fold the right sleeve as in (8b), but rest the raised sleeve directly on the head with the right arm gracefully poised in a curve just above the head as if to shelter it from scorching sun or heavy rain (Illus. 42).

Meaning: The sleeve serves as a shade.

12. THE RUNNING SLEEVES (掠 袖 Illus. 37).

Throw the sleeves upward and let them hang slanting on the outer side of the wrists. Then immediately stretch out both arms level with the shoulders. The actor is not permitted to run straight forward, but rather sidewise, so in running to the right front, he first turns a little towards the left, though his torso and face should be kept towards the right. The right hand is raised a little higher than the head as if leading towards the front. Then, with small, mincing steps, he runs gracefully in curves and finally exits. If the destination is in the opposite direction, the actor performs the same movement but in the opposite direction.

13. THE WEEPING SLEEVE (搵 袖).

Hold the upper corner of the left sleeve with the right hand (bare), and raise to the eyes, just near enough to seem that the actor is wiping away his tears with the sleeve.

Meaning: The sleeve serves as a handkerchief.

Illus. 38. The Responding Sleeve (by Mei Lan-fang)

14. THE RESPONDING SLEEVE (叠 袖).

Placing the right hand below the chest and a little to the front, by a quick circular wrist motion fold the sleeve so as to let it rest slanting from the wrist (Illus. 38). At the same time, the actor bends a little forward and says to the inferior, who is bowing before him, "Please get up," or "No more salutation."

Meaning: To show familiarity. When both hands are employed, it signifies utmost intimacy between the person greeted and the person greeting.

15. THE INTRODUCTION SLEEVE (點 絳 通 名 袖).

This movement is usually made at the beginning of the play when the actor portrays a powerful general, a person of great prestige, etc., and is about to proclaim some solemn orders. With many of his followers standing on either side, the actor advances to the centre front of the stage and stands facing about 30 degrees to the right. He holds up his left hand, with the folded sleeve resting on it, directly in front of his face. The right hand (bare) holds the lower corner of the left "R Sleeve." In this posture, the actor sings the "tien-chiang-ch'un" (點 絳 唇) tune.[1] Sometimes the left sleeve is raised before the actor steps out of the "Shang-ch'ang-mên," the entrance curtain. After the delivery of the "tien-chiang-ch'un" the actor announces the name of the character he is to play, while holding the sleeve as before, except lower down and before the chest.

Sometimes, instead of directly announcing his name, the actor performs a "la shan p'an" (see p. 116, Item 4) and then, raising the sleeve to the chest, introduces the character.

Meaning: To introduce the character to the audience. (The original meaning is that not until the sleeve is put down does the actor take up the rôle of the character in the play. In other words, before then he is the actor himself.)

---

[1] "Tien," "Chiang' and "Ch'un," the first three words in the song, were chosen as the title of that tune, because it was customary in Chinese drama to name a tune from the first three words. This tune is usually sung by those who impersonate high officials. It is similar to a prologue in nature.

Illus. 39.   The Attention Sleeve (by Ch'êng Yen-ts'iu)

16. THE RESTING SLEEVES (偏 袖).

Unless the actor plays the rôle of a ghost, or wishes to show that he is in a very awkward position, such as his conspiracy being discovered or his plan being utterly frustrated, he is forbidden to drop the hands to the sides of the body because this would be displeasing to the eye. Therefore, if one hand, for instance the right, is down a little to the left, the other should be placed on the right arm a little below the elbow (Illus. 72).

17. THE ATTENTION SLEEVE (揚 袖).

Raise the right hand to the side of the head and by a circular wrist movement fold the right sleeve upward and outward. Let it fall back, hanging naturally from the wrist, and at the same time say "Behold!" (Illus. 11, 39).

Meaning: (*a*)   To look ahead.

          (*b*)   To tell the person addressed to look ahead.

          (*c*)   To give a signal call (see "Chiao-pan," p. 79) to the orchestra.

18. THE FOLDING SLEEVE (折 袖).

First throw the sleeve upward so as to cause part of the "R Sleeve" to fold upon the wrist and rest on the back of the hand with the sleeve hanging down naturally (Illus. 58).

19. THE SNATCHED SLEEVE (抓 袖).

Swing the right sleeve inward and then outward. By a quick movement catch the sleeve in the right hand and hold the arm in a curve on the right side of the body, level with the chest (Illus. 40). This is usually performed by the military type characters, never by the "tan," but in the play "Loyalty Finds a Way," where the beautiful lady feigns insanity to avoid a second marriage, it is permitted in order to prove to the Emperor that she is insane.

20. THE HANGING SLEEVES (垂 袖).

When an actor plays the rôle of a ghost or the rôle of one in great distress, he extends his arms straight down, letting the sleeves hang a little to the front and about six inches from the body (Illus. 40).

Illus. 40. "Mang": (*Left to right*) 1—"Fun-lien" (by Liu Lien-yung);
The Hanging Sleeves. 2—"Shên" (by Wang Shau-t'ing).
3—"Tan" (by Mei Lan-fang); The Snatched Sleeve

PLAY: *Loyalty Finds a Way*

Illus. 41. The Dusting Sleeve (by the Author)

Illus. 42. The Shading Sleeve (by the Author)

Illus. 43.   The Upheld Sleeve; "Tieh-tzŭ" (by Yu Shu-yen, China's leading "Lao-shên"); The Open Hand; "Ch'ou" (by Wang Ch'ang-lin)

Illus. 44. (*Left to right*) 1—Long "K'an-chien" (the Maid by Chu Kuei-fang).
2—The Lady (by Mei Lan-fang). 3—The Open Hands; "Fun-lien"
(by Liu Lien-yung)

PLAY: *Loyalty finds a Way*

ℋand ℳovements

Next in importance to the sleeve movement is the hand movement, for in plays where the female impersonator takes the rôles of "hua-tan" and "kuei-mên-tan" or in dances where an article or articles, *e.g.* a plume or two swords, are held, the sleeves only reach to the ,wrist.

1.   THE OPEN HAND (張 手).

In stage language the "open" hand means that the palm is held outward with the finger-tips up. In case of a "tan" the arm should be held gracefully. Each character type, however, has its peculiar way of "opening" hands. For example:

(*a*) "Ch'in" (the painted-face characters): Extend the fingers with strength keeping them all apart so that the tips of the fingers form a semi-circle (Illus. 44).

(*b*) "Lao-shên" (the aged male characters): Extend the four fingers with the thumb bent forward at right angles to them (Illus. 90).

(*c*) "Hsiao-shên" (the young male characters): Extend and hold together the first three fingers, with the thumb bent close to the palm and the little finger, slightly forward and apart from the others.

97

Illus. 45.   The Helpless Hands (by Mei Lan-fang and Wang Shau-t'ing)

PLAY: *The Valiant Fisherman and His Daughter*

(*d*) "Tan" (the female characters): Put the thumb on the **last** joint of the middle finger which is held a little forward **and** leave the other three fingers naturally extended.

 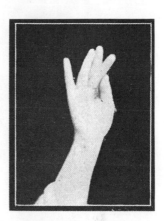

The Open Hand

2. THE HELPLESS HANDS (攤 手).

First lift both hands prone and by a quick circular wrist movement turn palms up, leaving the hands hanging limp from the wrists. Simultaneously, shake the head (Illus. 45).

Meaning: (*a*) To show helplessness.
(*b*) To show that something is lacking.

3. THE HINDERING HAND (攔 手).

Open the right hand as in (1), palm towards the left, in a defensive position and turn the head to the right. If the left hand is used, it should go through the same movements but in opposite direction. If both hands are raised at the same time, they should be held from one to one-and-a-half feet apart, with both palms in the same direction and the face turned away (Illus. 51).

Meaning: To hinder or to disapprove.

4. THE FIGHTING FIST (拳 手).

Bend the four fingers, and press the thumb tightly against **the** middle joint of the middle finger, with the index finger curved **above**

Illus. 46. The Contemplative or the Project Hand (by Mei Lan-fang)

the thumb. The tip of the little finger should touch the third finger, because a tight fist does not look artistic. This movement is seldom performed by "tan," but in the play "The Meeting at the Fallen Bridge" (see p. 215), the maid does often raise her fists against her supposed master in revenge for his desertion of the White Snake Lady, her mistress.

Meaning: To protest or to fight with fists.

5. THE YIELDING HANDS (战 手).

Lift the right hand as high as the face, palm outward in a defensive position, with the left hand resting, palm up, before the waist. Then move the right hand down in front while the left moves up. When the hands have completed the circle, the back of the right hand descends sharply into the left palm. Simultaneously, the right foot is slightly stamped to indicate the proper emotion.

Meaning:　(*a*)　To express disappointment.
　　　　　　(*b*)　To express regret.
　　　　　　(*c*)　To show that the person is compelled to reach a decision.

6. THE CONTEMPLATIVE HAND OR THE PROJECT HAND (想 計).

(*a*) Raise the left hand (bare) to the head; and place the middle finger on the temple, with eyes downcast and head drooping a little forward. Place the right hand at the back or with bare hand grasp the lower part of the left sleeve, folded on the forearm (Illus. 46).

(*b*) Place the right hand "open" on the chest. Move it in circles, with only the middle finger and the palm touching. At the same time, move the head in circles in harmony with the hand movements.

(*c*) Put the palms together before the chest. Slip the left hand down, and bend the four fingers of the right hand over those of the left, when the latter rests on the right palm. Repeat the above with right hand leading, and with head drooping slightly.

(*d*) Shake the head and clap the hands once. Lift the right hand to the head. Alternately tap the first two finger tips against the temple. Walk back and forth restlessly, looking downward and with the left hand moving in circles on the back of the left hip.

Illus. 47.   The Fencing Hand (by Mei Lan-fang)

PLAY: *The Filial Daughter, Lien Chin-fêng*

7. THE FENCING HAND (劍 訣).

This is the only time when a "tan" extends the first two fingers, instead of only the index finger. The thumb touches the third finger tip and the little finger is curved naturally (Illus. 47, 71):

8. THE ASIDE HAND (背 供 手).

Raise the hand sufficiently high to hide the face from the other characters on the stage and then express the emotion or secret to the audience (see the "aside" sleeve).

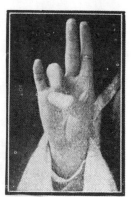

The Fencing Hand

9. THE SWIMMING HANDS (游 泳 手).

Extend the hands forward and then push the arms outward and backward as if swimming.

10. THE GESTURES OF POINTING (指 式).

There are many kinds of gestures to show direction. When an object is to be located, it is not permissible to point directly at it, but it is necessary to first move the pointing hand gracefully in curves or circles, before pointing. Generally for objects at a distance the pointing hand moves in larger rounds or curves than for objects near at hand. A "tan" should keep the following rules:

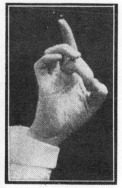

The tip of the thumb should lightly touch the middle finger tip with the index finger extended, and the other fingers curved naturally like orchid leaves. From this position of the hand the expression "Orchid-fingers" is derived.

The Harmony of Bodily Movements. If the right hand does the pointing, the eyes follow its movements and the whole body assumes a graceful, poised position with the right foot a little to the back, and the left hand akimbo or in front of

The Pointing Hand the lower chest. Every action must be done strictly

Illus. 48. (*Left to right*) 1—"Fun-lien" (by Liu Lien-yung); 2—"Tan" Pointing
Above (by Mei Lan-fang); 3—The Maid (by Chu Kuei-fang)

PLAY: *Loyalty Finds a Way*

according to the musical tempo. If the left hand points, the action is the same, but in the opposite direction. Usually, when an object at a distance is to be indicated, the body leans a little forward; if at a height, a little backward; if at a point diagonally left or right, a little towards that particular direction.

1. To point straight in front (前 指).

    (a) *On a high level.* The pointing hand starts slightly below the face, moves inward, makes a circle, and points toward the object with a prone hand (Illus. 48).

    (b) *On a low level.* The hand starts as in (a), but points below in front of the feet instead of above.

2. To point to the right front (右 指).

    (a) *On a high level.* The right hand starts three to four inches before the left shoulder, moves left and downward in a curve, and then up, pointing to the right with a prone hand.

    (b) *On a low level.* The right hand starts from high above the head, moves downward and to the left in a curve and then points outward and downward towards the right with a prone hand.

3. To point to the left front (左 指).

    (a) *On a high level.* The right hand starts at the same place as in (2a) but instead of moving to the left and downward, it moves upward in a left-to-right circle, and finally points to the left with palm at right angles to the floor (Illus. 49).

    (b) *On a low level.* The hand starts as in (2b), but moves downward to the right in a curve, and points to the left with a supine hand.

4. To point to the back (背 指).

There are three methods of performing this movement. The eyes, after following the hand movements, should immediately turn to the person with whom the performer is speaking.

    (a) After a circular wrist movement, the supine right hand points backward over the right shoulder.

Illus. 49.   Pointing to the Left Front (by Mei Lan-fang) ; "Lao-shên"
(by Wang Shau-t'ing)

PLAY: *The Suspicious Slipper*

(b) The right hand starts level with the left shoulder, or a little below the face, moves upward and outward in a circle and points through the left arm (akimbo) with a supine hand.

(c) The right hand starts before the left shoulder and moves upward and outward in a circle. On coming to the left shoulder again, the hand, now relaxed, should, by a graceful wrist movement, turn the palm toward the left and point backward over the left shoulder.

5. "Fan Chih" (翻 指) *i.e.* to point above or below with the hand above the head.

The right hand (prone) starts a little before the face and moves downward and toward the left in a circular movement. Gradually the arm is lifted until it is poised above the head in a curve with a supine hand pointing up (the head is now inclined toward the right front by the bending of the body in that direction). The left hand should be akimbo, and the right foot a little behind the left.

In pointing below, the upper part of the body should lean toward the left. Therefore, in both of the postures, the upheld arm is always at right angles to the head.

6. To point with both hands (雙 手 指).

When both hands are employed to point at the same time, the "leading" hand is about one foot from the "following" hand, in a slanting line to the body, with the foot on the opposite side a little to the rear. If the right hand is leading, the left foot steps back simultaneously as the hand points to the definite object or direction. The eyes should follow the movement of the hands and the body should be held in harmony with them.

Sometimes, however, the hands may point alternately, and in that case, they move in the direction to be indicated, in successive advancing circles.

7. To point in hate or in anger (怒 指).

The actor follows the directions as in (1*a*), but points directly at the person hated, and accompanies the act with the proper facial expression.

Illus. 50.   Pointing to Oneself   (by Mei Lan-fang)

PLAY: *A Nun Seeks Love*

8. To point at a group of objects (橫 指).

Start with right hand, palm upward, a little below the left shoulder, move it toward the right in a horizontal line to about two feet from the starting point. Actors playing rôles other than "tan" point with a prone hand.

The gestures described above refer only to the location of other persons or things. The following explain those gestures which locate the parts of one's own body:

9. To point to oneself (自 指).

(a) Place the hands (bare) "open" (see p. 99), palms upward, against the chest, with the fingers of one hand above those of the other. At the same time nod the head once as if in acknowledgment.

(b) Raise the right hand (bare) "open," and place the extended middle finger on the chest, palm toward the body (Illus. 50) and nod.

(c) If the actor wears long sleeves, the right hand should be similarly placed before the chest, with the sleeve previously folded by an upward and outward turn at the wrist.

10. To point to the head (指 頭).

Start with the right hand a little in front of the left shoulder and move it outward and downward in a curve. Then gradually lift the arm and when the elbow is about level with the shoulder on the right side, point to the head with a supine hand.

11. To point to the face or any part of the face (指面或口鼻等).

There are three different ways of doing this:

(a) For the right side, point with the right hand, palm outward, about three inches distance from, and on the level with the part of the face to be indicated. For the left side, use the left hand.

(b) Same as in (a) as to the position of the hand with regard to the face, except that the hand is held "open," palm inward, without using the index finger for pointing.

Illus. 51.   The Hindering Hand ("Tan" by Mei Lan-fang); "Wu-ch'in"
(by Liu Lien-yung); The Maids on the sides (by Yao Yü-fu
and Chu Kuei-fang)

(c) Reach forth the right hand to the left side (or the left hand to the right) about level with the left shoulder, palm outward, and point with the index finger backward toward the face.

12. To point to the arm (or the hand 指 胳 膊 或 手).

Raise the arm (or the hand) to be indicated in a curve before the chest, palm outward, hand "open." Then similarly hold up the other hand, also palm outward, with the index finger pointing to the arm (or the hand).

13. To point to the waist (指 腰).

All characters other than "tan" never point to the waist but indicate it by putting the hands on it, because it is considered vulgar to point to the waist. Only a "tan" may put her hand across and point to the other side of the waist; for instance, a "tan" may extend the right hand across the front and point to the left side of the waist.

14. To point to the leg (or the foot 指 腿 或 足).

Place the right foot behind and a little to the left of the other foot. Extend the right hand across the front, and point a little backward to the right leg (or the right foot) with a supine hand, held at the left side of the waist. Turn the head to the left, with eyes following the movements of the hand. The left hand may be held either akimbo or in a curve before the chest.

15. To point to the chest or the abdomen (指 胸 或 腹).

It is strictly forbidden to directly point to the chest or the abdomen, for such movement is very unpleasing to the eye. An actor, however, may lightly touch these parts, if the indication is necessary.

Besides the above mentioned ways of pointing, there are still others, such as to point with the object held in the hand and to point with an empty hand to the object held in the other hand.

16. To point with an object, such as a fan, a horse-whip (see p. 24, Item 4), a duster (see Footnote, "A Nun Seeks Love"), a pen, a sword or a sabre (持 物 件 指 一).

The object is usually held with the thumb and the first two fingers, leaving the other fingers naturally curved or artistically extended (Illus.

Illus. 52. Pointing to the Object Held in the Other Hand ("Tan" by Mei Lan-fang);
"Lao-shên" (by Wang Shau-t'ing)

PLAY: *The Suspicious Slipper*

50, 51, 52). The other parts of the body should also be kept in harmony with the hand movements, as above described. The following are the three ways of pointing with the object:

 (*a*) Hold the handle of the object and point with its head.

 (*b*) Hold the handle of the object (palm downward) with the third and fourth fingers in such a position that the object's head hangs down and the index finger points the direction.

 (*c*) Hold the handle, letting the object rest on the arm and point with the index finger of the same hand.

 17. To point with an empty hand to the object held in the other hand (持 物 件 指 二).

 (*a*) The object is held level with the shoulder.

Raise the pointing hand upward and to the right in a curve. When a circle is completed, point with palm outward (Illus. 52). Or, raise the pointing hand a little before the shoulder, move it outward and downward in a small circle and point to the object with a supine hand.

 (*b*) The object is poised on the fingers of one hand in front of and above the shoulder.

The pointing hand starts a little in front of the chest and about level with the shoulder, and moves in a right-to-left circle (if the right hand is pointing) or vice versa if the left hand is pointing. The arm is gradually lifted a little above the head, and toward the front in a curve, the hand pointing to the object with the palm outward.

 18. To point with an open fan (持 張 扇 指).

Besides the above mentioned ways of pointing with an object, a "tan," and only a "tan," has two other methods of indicating direction by the use of an open fan. For example, in pointing to the right:

 (*a*) Hold the open fan in a horizontal position in the right hand a little below the right shoulder with the outside corner of the fan pointing to the right. The left hand should slightly touch the inner edge of the fan.

 (*b*) Hold the fan in the left hand as in (*a*), and rest the right hand on it. Then after going through the necessary circular movements, the right hand points to the right.

19. To point to a city gate (指 城 門).

This is a special movement, performed only for this purpose. There are usually three characters in the name of a city and these are placed over the gate (see p. 25, Item 13).

The hand must point three times. Each time the actor points, he reads a character. If he reads the name twice, he must point six times.

Arm Movements

As some of the arm movements have been described in Chapters
I and II, the following descriptions will only cover those in which the
hands move similarly to those already described but in which the
position of the arms is different.

1. THE EMBRACING ARMS (抱 胳 膊)

Fold the forearms across the chest, letting the palms rest on the
upper arms. Sometimes, slightly shake the head.
Meaning: (*a*)   To show despair.
             (*b*)   To express chilliness or illness.

2. THE RESTING ARMS (垂 胳 膊).

Only those characters playing the rôle of a ghost are permitted to
let their arms hang at their sides. Even those who play servants and
stand in waiting at the sides of the stage should slightly bend one arm
and place the hand on the hanging arm a little below the elbow (see
"resting" sleeves, p. 91). A person, however, feeling very awkward
may let his hands hang down stiffly, but they must not rest against the
body (Illus. 40).

3. "YUIN SHOU," A DANCING POSTURE (雲 手).

This is one of the postures from the T'ang dance. It is usually
connected with and followed by a "La Shan P'an" (see p. 116).

115

Start with the left hand (palm up) below the right (palm down). Move the left hand inward and to the right, and the right hand outward and to the left in horizontal circles. Sometimes this is performed together with a rotation of the body.

4. "LA SHAN P'AN," ANOTHER DANCING POSTURE (拉 山 髈).

This and the preceding posture have been transmitted directly from the dance without alteration. They are performed by the acrobatic characters whenever they start to do some act or to finish some fancy movement before their exit.

Turn the body from the waist up a little to the right. Raise the left arm in a curve with "open" hand before the chest. Raise the right arm with the hand also "open" and hold before the left shoulder about three inches from the left hand, both palms outward. Extend the left arm to the left with the hand in "fist" (see p. 99, Item 4) and lastly extend the right hand to the right, with eyes following. Poise both arms level with the shoulders.

Foot Movements

The foot movement is no less important than that of the hand, because it is also developed from the ancient dance. Every single step, either in stage walking or running, must be performed in accord with the music. There are different rules for the gait of the various character types. Moreover, an actor has to observe different rules of acting when different costumes are worn, even in the same play.

The table on the following page illustrates these rules.

There are as many kinds of foot movements as there are of sleeve movements, but only the more important ones often performed by the "tan" are described here:

1. THE STAGE WALKING (正 步).

The female characters should walk in shorter steps than the male. The quicker the pace, the shorter the step. In the shortest step, the toe of the leading foot is only three to four inches ahead of the rear foot. In a long step, the sole of the leading foot should be placed one to two inches before the toe of the rear one. The feet should be kept close together, the utmost distance apart not exceeding two inches. In brief, while advancing, the feet should move so that the toes are almost even.

2. THE STAGE RUNNING (跑 步).

The body above the waist should be kept very steady. Faster running demands shorter steps, in order that the appearance of speed

117

BODY MOVEMENTS OF THE VARIOUS CHARACTERS IN THEIR RESPECTIVE COSTUMES.

CHARACTERS / COSTUMES	"Tan," the female rôle	"Lao-shên," the dignified old man	"Hsiao-shên," the young man	"Ch'ou," the clown	"Ch'in," the painted face character
"Mang," the robe, with "Yü-tai," the belt (see p. 19 Items 1 and 2)	Body straight / Hands on belt / Walk in dignified manner	Body same / Hands same / Walk in "square" strides	Body same / Hands same / Feet lifted forward high enough for the audience to see the bottom of the boots	Body a little forward / Hands same / Walk in undignified manner	Body very straight / Hands same / Walk in broad strides, with feet very much apart
"P'ei," the overcoat (see p. 21, Item 4)	Body and head movement free / Walk with feet near together / Knees a little bent	Body slightly forward / Walk in less "square" strides	Body rather straight / Walk in slightly "square" strides	Body swaying / Same as "hsiao-shên"	Body straight / Walk with toes turned outward
"Tieh-tzŭ," the everyday apparel (see p. 19, Item 3)	Body and head movement very free / Walk with short steps / Hands in "resting" sleeves	Body same / Motions free	Body same / Walk in swaying strides / Motions very free	Body a little forward and swaying / Walk in small steps	Body same only torso erect / Walk in broad strides
"K'ai-k'ao," the armour with "K'ao-ch'i," the military flags (see pp. 21-22 Items 9 and 10)	Torso very erect so that the military flags will not strike each other / Arms flexed and extended somewhat from the body	Body straight / Walk in broad strides, thighs raised high	Same as "lao-shên"	Same as "lao-shên," only movements more free	Body more stiff / Walk in long and broad strides

may be given while in reality the degree of advancement is very low. Sometimes a "tan" may run with a "shading" sleeve instead of "running" sleeves. It is not permissible to let the skirt fly out, for it looks less graceful and elegant.

Throughout the world actions on the stage are not supposed to be exactly the same as those in daily life, but in Chinese plays the difference is more striking than in the plays of any other country. The conventional gait must be in keeping with each particular character in the play. Therefore, we have the short, graceful, mincing steps of "tan," the round or square strides of "shên," etc. The only thing that is common to all characters is that all actors must keep perfect step in harmony with the music.

3. THE STAGGERING STEPS (暈 步).

To represent an intoxicated person or one who is weak from illness, the actor steps with the right foot to the side (or front or back), letting the weight of his body fall on it. Then, almost immediately, he steps again and throws his whole weight on the left foot. Simultaneously the neck and the arms are relaxed. Repeat as many times as necessary.

4. THE SLIPPING STEP (滑 步).

To represent a wet and muddy street, the actor, usually in running, performs "the slip" by extending one foot forward and bending the other, with the body falling backward and resting on the bent leg.

5. THE UP-STAIRS AND DOWN-STAIRS STEPS (上 樓 步 — 下 樓 步).

(a) Bend the body slightly forward; lift the front of the skirt a little; raise the thigh in stepping, as if the person were ascending real stairs. Each step should be about four to five inches in length.

(b) Bend as in (a); lift the side of the skirt a little; raise the right thigh, but less than in (a). Bend the left knee when the right foot steps down, as if descending real stairs.

6. THE KNEE-STEPS (膝 行 步).

This is mostly done by actors playing female rôles.

(a) Raise both sleeves as in "upheld" sleeves; walk either forward or sidewise on the knees.

(*b*)   Raise one sleeve, and with the other hand resting on another person, walk on the knees.

7.   THE STANDING POSTURE (踏 步).

(*a*)   Stand on one foot with the other nearly behind it, or with the toe of the other foot barely touching the floor.

(*b*)   Stand with the toe of one foot close beside the middle of the other and with the knees pressed together, so as to facilitate the swaying of the body.

8.   THE STAMPING (頓 足).

In regret or despair, the stamping is done similarly to that in everyday life, except that it is always accompanied by the "yielding hands." Every character should stamp on the "pan" (板), *i.e.* the stroke of the "time beater" (see p. 32, Item 7), the player of which serves as the orchestral director. The military character type brings down the foot very forcibly, while a "tan" always stamps delicately.

9.   THE JUMPING STEPS (趨 步).

Step forward on the right foot and, as it touches the floor, spring forward on the left foot, simultaneously raising the right to the front, toe downward. Repeat as many times as necessary.

Sometimes, alternate jumping steps (三 趨 步) are performed by going through the following motions:

Step forward on the right foot with arms in curves before the chest, the left arm leading, and jump with the left, as in the above described "jumping." Then as the right foot rests on the floor, the left steps forward, with the right arm leading. Jump forward on the right foot, with the left raised to the front. Repeat, with the right foot again leading.

Meaning: Originally it meant to hurry. Now it is no longer limited to its old meaning, but is often performed as a fancy movement.

10.   THE SIDEWISE STEPS, No. I (跨 步).

Hold the body erect with legs close together; step right foot sidewise, about two to three inches. Follow quickly with the left; and again advance on the right foot.   Both feet should be kept so close to the floor that they seem not to leave it.

Meaning: Originally it meant "unable to advance, yet compelled to progress."   It is one of the movements made by the White Snake Lady in the play "The Golden Mountain Monastery." (see p. 213).

11.   THE SIDEWISE STEPS, No. II (輾 步).

In this movement, it is forbidden to move the whole foot forward. Start with toes together and the feet forming an angle of sixty degrees. If going to the right, the actor should move the right toe and the left sole to the right at the same time.   As soon as they rest on the floor move the right sole and the left toe very quickly.   Repeat as long as required.

Meaning: Same as No. I: This movement is often performed because of the beauty of the motion.

12   THE MINCING STEPS (蹉 步).

Keep the feet close together, and advance in quick, short steps, not more than two inches in length.   This is usually performed by the sprightly, coquettish "hua-tan" type.

Meaning: Anxious to advance, yet for some reason or other it seems impossible to hasten.

Sometimes, this action may be performed in retreat.   In this case, it is called the "mincing-retreat" step (倒 蹉 步).

Meaning: The character is on horseback and the horse getting stubborn refuses to advance.

13.   THE GHOST STEPS (魂 子 步).

With the body very erect and stiff and with arms and hands hanging, walk smoothly in very short steps so as not to rustle the costume.   To represent taking a distant trip, the ghost character whirls around three times, for it is believed that when ghosts travel, they ride on whirlwinds.

Meaning: To represent a ghost on a journey.

14. THE CROSS STEP (十字步)

Place the left foot at right angles to and about twelve inches in front of the right foot. Simultaneously raise the hands, the left to the back, the right to the front, and higher. Then advance with the right foot and left hand leading. This movement may be seen in the play "The Golden Mountain Monastery."

Meaning: It is a dancing posture.

15. THE SIDEWISE CROSS STEP (連三步).

It is usually done with partners facing each other. In going to the left side, cross the right foot over the left. Then move the left into place. Repeat the movement.

It may also be done by first raising the right leg high, and then kicking out to the left before putting the foot down. Advance to the left by repeating the same movement.

Meaning: To show excitement. The character is so excited that his actions are uncontrollable.

16. THE GET-ABOARD STEP (躦步)

Raise the left foot high and spring forward with a long step. Before the left foot reaches the floor, raise the right foot a little to the rear. When the left foot rests on the floor, the right foot is placed against the left leg without touching the floor. This is usually followed by quick running.

Meaning: To go aboard a boat or ship hurriedly.

Leg Movements

There are many kinds of leg movements which an apprentice must begin learning while very young, for otherwise he will be unable to master the balancing of the body gracefully. As leg and foot movements are inseparable, a number of the leg movements as auxiliary to foot movements were described in the last chapter. In the present chapter only those movements in which the foot does not touch the floor are described.

1. THE STANDING POSTURE (蹲 腿).

The most important rule in Chinese drama is that actors when standing always have one or both knees slightly flexed.
Meaning: (a) To show readiness to move gracefully.
  (b) To avoid stiffness, especially for the "tan."

2. THE FLEXED KNEE (彎 腿).

Stand erect on the right foot, lift the left thigh to a horizontal position, and hold the lower leg so as to form an obtuse angle. This movement is usually performed by the military character type.
Meaning: To show alertness.

3. THE LIFTED LEG (提 腿).

Lift the thigh as high as possible, but keep the toe extended downward.
Meaning: To show readiness to kick.

Illus. 53. Turning on Horseback (by Mei Lan-fang)

4. Turning on Horseback (跨 腿)

(*a*) If the right leg is used to perform this movement, raise it to the side (because the actor is supposed to be on horseback) with thigh in horizontal position and the lower leg slanting toward left front.   The left arm should be akimbo or extended to the left, level with the shoulder, and the right arm and hand curved in front of the waist (left) thumb down, palm outward, holding the whip, tip up (Illus. 53).

(*b*) If with the left leg, first raise it as in (*a*) but keep the toe down.   Hold the arms in curves before the waist with the hands in "fists" as if reining up the horse.

When a "tan" rides the leg is slightly raised, it not being permissible for that character type to lift the leg high.

Meaning: This movement is performed only when the rider makes a turn in direction.

5. The Kicking Foot or Leg (踢 腿).

Formerly, a "tan" was not allowed to kick, but recently this restriction has been removed when she plays a military rôle.   Raise the thigh as in (2), kick out with strength to the right (or the left).   The body must be held steadily erect, for even its slight swaying spoils the poise.

6. The Exit Posture (抬 腿).

This is a dancing posture for leaving the stage; therefore, the performer faces the "Hsia-ch'ang-mên" (the exit curtain).   He stands erect with the weight on the right foot and raises the left thigh high, with the lower leg slanting to the right, toe down.   He curves the left arm in front of the chest and extends the right to the side, level with shoulder, hand either "open" or with a whip (see p. 24, Item 4), tip up.   He looks toward the "Hsia-ch'ang-mên" (Illus. 54).

Illus. 54.   The Exit Posture; Leading a "Horse" (by Mei Lan-fang)

Waist Movements

Every movement of the waist when dancing must be exceedingly pliant and graceful. We can see how imperiously flexibility of the waist is required by the frequent use of the term "willowy waist" in describing a lady's form.

As the waist nearly always moves in harmony with the limbs and as its movements have also been mentioned in the preceding chapters, the following two movements in which only the waist moves will be described. Both of them demand an early start in learning and unceasing practice ever afterwards, for an actor can never succeed otherwise.

1. A Low Bend (下 腰).

Stand facing the audience, bend backward with a very flexible waist so as to make the body look like an elegant arch.

2. A Kite's Turn (彎腰 或 鷂子 翻身).

Bend backward and to the right (or left) with the arms akimbo. Turn with the body, thus bent, from right to left or vice versa. This movement demands strong legs and a graceful waist. It is best portrayed in "The Intoxicated Beauty, Yang Kuei-fei". The actor bends back to the right low enough to grasp the wine cup on the servant's tray with his teeth, turns his body, thus bent, to the left as if he were drinking the wine from the cup and then drops the cup on the tray held by the servant on the left.

Illus. 55.   Holding the Pheasant Feather; "Chih-vei-hsiao-shên"
(by Lee Wan-ch'un)

CHAPTER
SEVEN

Pheasant Feather Movements

Originally the pheasant feathers on the headdress, the longest of which was seven or eight feet in length, indicated that the wearer was a robber chieftain, a barbarian general, or a general fighting against the imperial house. Later, on account of the beauty of the feathers, the Chinese generals began to wear them too. Actors playing the rôle of young or female generals usually wear them because of their pleasing appearance. Moreover, later actors have invented so many methods of dancing with the feathers that a special class of motions has been gradually developed.

While in the other movements the "tan" acts differently from the other character types, in these, all actors perform the same, except that a "ch'in" (the painted-face character) holds the feathers higher than either a "lao-shên" (the aged male character) or a "hsiao-shên" (the young male character), and a "tan" poises them a little above the shoulders.

1. Winding the Feathers (繞 翎).

Drop the head forward and turn it in a circular movement with a relaxed neck so that the feathers move in large circles. The prettiest way of performing this movement is to make the circuit of the feathers perfectly round.

Meaning: To show anger or determination.

129

Illus. 56. "K'ai-k'ao" and "K'ao-ch'i"; Dancing with the Pheasant
Feathers (by Mei Lan-fang)

2. NODDING WITH THE FEATHERS (栽 翎).

Bend forward with the head hung so low that the feather tips touch the floor. Then raise the head. It seems a very simple movement, but the actor must have both tips raised or touching the floor at the same time.
Meaning: To show surprise, contemplation or recollection.

3. PLAYING WITH THE FEATHERS (耍 翎).

Bend forward at the waist, drop the head a little to the side front, so that one feather goes forward touching the floor and the other goes backward. Lift the head and again drop forward, reversing the order. It is very hard to do this movement satisfactorily.

4. HOLDING THE FEATHER, No. I (持 翎).

The feather is held between the index and the middle fingers so that when the hand turns, it follows in curves. The test of the actor's skill lies in the roundness of the curves. The feather is never held otherwise, lest it be injured by pressure of the fingers.

Raise the right hand to the feather; let it slip through the fingers until they are about a foot from the tip. Then by a circular wrist motion, move the hand inward in a horizontal circle, poising it, palm toward the right, feather tip up, on the right and a little higher than the head. The left hand usually holds something. If not, it should be akimbo. The eyes, after following the hand should look up (Illus. 55).
Meaning: To look far ahead.

5. HOLDING THE FEATHER, No. II (雙 持 翎).

Follow the same directions as in (4), but use both hands.
Turn the body toward the right and laugh aloud, then toward the left and laugh, and again toward the right and laugh.
Meaning: To show mirth with pride, *e.g.* a victorious general usually performs this movement before exit.

6. HOLDING THE FEATHER BETWEEN THE TEETH (啣 翎).

This is usually performed when the actor has an object, *e.g.* a spear or a sword, in one hand. Use the empty hand—say, the right—to place

Illus. 57. 'Dancing with the Pheasant Feathers (by Mei Lan-fang)

the feather between the teeth at a point from about six inches to one foot from the tip.   Then pass the object to the right hand and hold the feather in the left as in (4).

Sometimes both feathers are held between the teeth, but this movement is usually performed when the hands are empty and long sleeves are worn.

Meaning: To show strong determination.

7.   DANCING WITH FEATHERS (舞 翎).

There are many ways of performing this movement, but only four have been selected.   They are usually performed by "tan" while walking or running in fancy steps (see "sidewise" steps) to show light-heartedness and joy; "hsiao-shên" (the young male character) does it too, only not so often as "tan."

(*a*)   Hold the feathers as in (5).   Start with both hands in front of the chest.   Move the left hand inward, and the right outward, in consecutive circles.   It is not permissible to move both hands inward or outward at the same time.

(*b*)   Hold the feathers as in (5).   Raise the right hand, palm out, to the right front, a little higher than the head, and place the left hand, palm down, either to the left side level with and one foot from the waist, or, with the forearm in a horizontal position, at the front of the chest (Illus. 56).   Sometimes, the actor may poise like this:

With the face and torso inclined to the right, extend the left foot across the right in front and either rest it there or raise it, toe down.

(*c*)   Hold the feathers and move the hands as in "Yuin Shou" (see p. 115), while turning the body in a right-to-left circle or vice versa.

(*d*)   Start with the feathers held at the front of the chest.   Move the right hand inward and downward and almost immediately move the left hand similarly.   When they have completed their circles, poise the right hand, palm out, level with the shoulder and the left, palm slanting toward the right front, level with or a little higher than the head.   Eyes follow the movements of the hands (Illus. 57).

Meaning: To show lightness and gaiety.

Illus. 58. The Dead Body; (*left*) The Upheld Sleeve; (*right*) The
Folding Sleeve (by Mei Lan-fang)

CHAPTER EIGHT

Some Symbolic Actions

I. To Look For Some Person or Object at A Distance (望 門) or Wang Men

(a) *Ahead.* Stand facing the "Hsia-ch'ang-mên" (the exit curtain), with a right (never left) "attention" sleeve.

(b) *Behind.* Stand facing the "Shang-ch'ang-mên" (the entrance curtain), with a left (never right) "attention" sleeve.

(c) *Direction uncertain.* The actor walks to the left side of the stage, performs (b), and turns facing the audience with "helpless" hands, showing that the person or object it not there. He then walks to the right and performs (a). These movements may be done in the reverse order.

II. The Dead Body (殭 屍) or Chiang Shih

To play fainting, the actor should fall back into a chair, body very stiff (Illus. 58).

III. To Prepare the Pen[1] For Writing (彈 墨) or Tan Me

The right hand picks up the pen; then with thumb and middle finger of the left hand remove any loosened hair from the brush, and flick it.

---

[1] A Chinese pen has nothing in common with a foreign pen. It is made of a bamboo holder and a brush of feathers or wool, or the hair of deer, wolf or a special kind of rat. During the Ch'ing Dynasty (A.D. 1644-1911), sable fur pens were used by the Imperial families. Sometimes it is necessary to point the brush before writing by flicking off the loosened hair from the brush so as to make the writing smooth. In Chinese plays, however, the actor does the flicking simply to give the orchestral director warning that he is ready to sing.

IV. CROSSING A THRESHOLD (跨門檻) OR K'UA MEN CHIEN

The actor lifts his right foot high as if he were stepping over the sill. On putting his weight on the right foot, the left is lifted backward before stepping over. Then he has either entered or left the house. (The threshold in the old-fashioned Chinese house is usually high, ranging from eight to twenty inches.)

V. THE SEDAN-CHAIR RIDE (乘轎) OR CH'ENG CHIAO

A "chang-tzǔ" (the big, embroidered curtain), held up on two poles by an actor stands for a bridal chair (or an ordinary sedan chair). The "rider" walks inside this curtain.

When men, usually of the official class, play riding in chairs, there are often four to eight servants standing on the sides of the stage. The leading servant first walks forward, stands facing the master, raises his right or left hand (depending upon their standing positions), and moves it sidewise in a big curve as if he were raising the curtain of the chair. At the same time the rider stoops a little forward and steps backward two or three feet, does the pantomime of sitting down, before he advances, as if he were entering the chair and then riding forward in it.

On reaching the destination, the servant goes through the same pantomime of pushing aside the curtain to let the rider out, while the latter again stoops, and then steps forward as if he were getting out of the chair.

VI. HOW TO OPEN AND CLOSE A DOOR (OR A WINDOW) (開閉門窗) OR KAI PI MEN CH'UANG

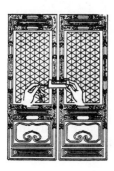

1. *To open a locked door from outside.* Use the thumb and index finger of the left hand, palm outward, as if holding the lock, open it with the right hand as if putting in the key. Then remove the lock; put hands together, palm outward, and push them forward and apart with body gradually inclining forward as if pushing the doors apart.

For unlocked doors, omit the lock-removing movements.

2. *To open from inside.* (*a*) The main double door: Hold the left palm outward, and the thumb and the first two fingers of the right hand as if they were grasping the bolt (horizontal fastening). Move the "bolt" to the right. With hands together in front, draw them inward as if pulling open the doors. Walk toward the left with hands raised, palms outward, as if pushing back the heavy left door. Repeat the movement for the right door.

(*b*) The ordinary double door: Start as in (2*a*) only after removing the "bolt," push the "doors" back at the same time. Since they are not heavy portals, it is unnecessary to use both hands. If a single door is to be represented, push it back with the right hand.

3. *To close from outside.* Cross the threshold as in (IV); turn back; step with right foot over the "doorsill" and draw the left "door" with the right hand, while stepping back. Similarly close the right "door" with the left hand. Pull the "doors" into place and "lock." Doors of smaller size may be shut at the same time.

4. *To close from inside.* Follow the same directions as in (2*a*) and (2*b*) only instead of pushing, pull the doors into place, and instead of removing the "bolts," bolt them. In short, reverse the actions in (2*a*) and (2*b*).

Windows are opened or closed as in (2*b*) and (4) but with hands raised, as window fastenings are supposed to be rather high.

The poor are represented as living in caves, the entrance of which is very low, hence there is a special method for entering and leaving such an abode:

5. *Coming out.* Stoop down, remove the "bolt" and open the door with the right hand, palm outward, and with the left hand helping or in front of the chest. Fold the right sleeve, step out with stooped body. Stand erect and perform a "turning" sleeve.

6. *Entering.* Fold the right sleeve as in the "folding" sleeve, stoop very low with back toward the audience; step into the cave; turn facing the audience, push leftward the right hand, "open," palm outward, as if closing the door. Raise the left hand, also "open" and palm outward, level with the chin as if leaning on the door frame. With the right hand perform the pantomime of holding the "bolt" and moving it to the left as if bolting the door. Then stand up.

Illus. 59. The "Heart-protecting Glass"; Mounting an Imaginary Horse
(by Mei Lan-fang)

PLAY: *Mu-lan, the Disguised Warrior Maiden*

These movements are portrayed in "The Suspicious Slipper" (see story). In that play, the male character, to show that he has grown unaccustomed to entering such wretched lodgings, does the pantomime of bumping his forehead on the "beam" above the "door."

VII.   To Mount an Imaginary Horse (上 馬) or Shang Ma

1.   Raise the right hand "open" as if to stroke the "horse."

2.   Close the left hand as if to hold the "reins."

3.   Pass the third finger of the right hand into the loop of the whip (see p. 24, Item 4) handle.   Then the hand clasps the handle.

4.   As the whip is drawn back, the left foot is lifted to the "stirrup" (Illus. 59).

5.   As the whip descends on the back, the right foot is thrown across the "saddle."

6.   As the rider is seated, the left hand tightens the "reins."

7.   The rider now faces the audience with an uplifted whip, ready to set out on the journey (Illus. 61).

VIII.   To Dismount an Imaginary Horse (下 馬) or Hsia Ma

1.   Move the right arm and hand with whip up and toward the right in a big circle and then hold the whip horizontally in front with the left hand touching the tip of the whip.   Simultaneously, look at the audience as if saying, "I have reached my destination."

2.   By a circular wrist movement turn the whip downward and to the right.   When the circle is completed, slip the little finger out of the loop, and pass the whip to the left hand.   Simultaneously, lift the right foot as if the rider were dismounting.

3.   While the left hand does the pantomime of gathering the "reins" and receiving the whip, the left foot steps as if getting out of the "stirrup."

4.   The whip is replaced in the right hand "to be led away" by the rider's servant.   Sometimes, the whip is thrown on the side of the stage meaning that the horse is let loose to graze.

Illus. 60.   Reining up a "Horse"

PLAY: *The Rainbow Pass*

IX. To Rein up an Imaginary Horse (勒 韁) or Le Chiang

The rider on horseback moves the whip backward and downward in a curve. When a circle is completed, he holds the whip in front of him with a prone hand (Illus. 21, 60).

X. To Lead an Imaginary Horse (牽 馬) or Ch'ien Ma

To lead a "horse" the actor holds the whip vertically by the handle, with its tip either up or down (Illus. 54).

When the "horse" is handed over to the rider, the whip is held horizontally, with the handle toward the latter. The right hand is extended to the side, and level with the shoulder. The actor in doing this should stand in front of and with his back towards the rider.

XI. How to Take a Seat (內 外 場 坐 法) or Nui Wai Ch'ang Ts'o Fa

The table at the centre of the stage serves as the demarcation line between "Wai Ch'ang Ts'o Wê" (外 場 坐 位 seat on the outer stage)

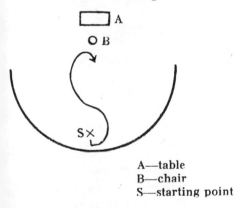

A—table
B—chair
S—starting point

and "Nui Ch'ang Ts'o Wê" (內 場 坐 位 seat on the inner stage). There are definite rules for the actor to follow when he is to take the Wai Ch'ang or Nui Ch'ang seat.

1. *To take a Wai Ch'ang seat* (坐 外 場):
First make the declamation at the front centre of the stage, turn left; walk in the direction of the arrow, forming the letter "S." On reaching the chair, turn right face and sit.

2. *To take a Nui Ch'ang seat* (坐 內 場):
Turn right face after declamation and walk in the direction of the arrow, forming the shape of a reverse "S." On reaching the table and the chair, turn left face and sit.

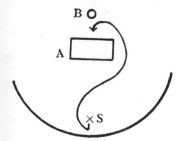

Illus. 61. Starting on Horseback (by Mei Lan-fang)

PLAY: *The Rainbow Pass*

XII. How a Host Seats His Guest (挖 門) or Wa Men

As it is rather difficult to describe the movements in mere words, the following figures may enable the reader to get a clearer idea.

1. *When the host and the guest enter through different doors:*

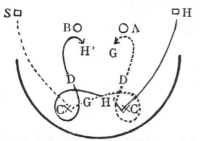

S—Shang-ch'ang-mên.
H—Hsia-ch'ang-mên.
A—Seat of Honour.
B—Seat of Host.
H'—Host.
G—Guest.
C—First Greeting Place.
D—Second Greeting Place.

The guest comes on the stage through S, while the host enters through H. They are to greet each other at C. Then they walk in the direction of the arrows until they come to D where they again exchange greetings, the host asking the guest to take A and the guest modestly refusing. Finally they proceed and take their seats.

2. *When the host and the guest enter through the same door:*

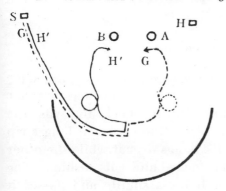

S—Shang-ch'ang-mên.
H—Hsia-ch'ang-mên.
A—Seat of Honour.
B—Seat of Host.
H'—Host.
G—Guest.

Through S the host leads the guest to the front centre of the stage, crosses the threshold and turns left toward S, while the guest goes right. They greet each other and proceed as in (1).

XIII. To Show a Person Under Arrest (被 捕) or Pei P'u

A character wearing a long string or silk band on the neck, with ends hanging down in the front, shows that he is under arrest.

XIV.   To Show a View Through a Prison Window (獄窗外望) or Yu Ch'uang Wai Wang

To show peeping through the window in the entrance gate of the prison, the character, playing jailor, stands at the back of a chair, and stoops to peep out through the space between the slats.

XV.   Admission Into a Prison (進牢) or Tsin Lao

The jailor who stands at the back of the chair, tilts the chair sidewise (meaning the prison door is opened) and then steps a little to the side so as to let the prisoner (or his friend or relative) enter.

XVI.   A Siege (被困) or Pei K'un

1.   *A Besieged City.*   Players run in big curves across the stage in opposite directions, *i.e.* those who come on the stage through the "Shang-ch'ang-mên" (or entrance curtain) go out through the "Hsia-ch'ang-mên" (or exit curtain) and vice versa.   A city wall (see p. 25, Item 13) is represented at the back centre of the stage.

2.   *A Besieged Family or Group of Men.*   Actors run as in (1) only instead of a city wall, the besieged group stands in the centre facing the back of the stage.

XVII.   Weaving (織布) or Chih Pu

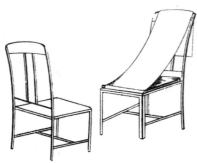

Chairs for a weaving scene

To represent weaving, the actor sits on one chair and faces another chair with its back towards the audience.   One end of a long strip of silk hangs over it while the other end is tucked under its cushion.   The actor holds a shuttle and passes it under and out from the stretched silk as if he were weaving cloth.

XVIII.   To Get Aboard a Boat (上船) or Shang Ch'uan

The actor jumps forward and while resting on the floor his body sways gracefully back and forth, in harmony with the up and down movements in the knees, as if to balance himself on the unsteady boat. Then he picks up the oar, placed on one side of the stage.

If two or more actors are in the boat, the leading one after getting aboard holds out his oar horizontally towards the other, as if to provide him with a support.

If an actor comes on stage through "Hsia-ch'ang-mên" (the exit curtain) with an oar in his hand, it usually means that he is already on the boat and is welcoming some passengers.   In this case, he holds out the oar, like the leading actor above-mentioned, towards those who enter through the "Shang-ch'ang-mên" (the entrance curtain).

XIX.   To Anchor a Boat (泊 船) or Pe Ch'uan

The actor after gracefully running in circles with an oar in his hand as if he were rowing, first places the oar on the floor and jumps two or three steps forward as if getting ashore.   Then he turns about face, stoops down, and does the pantomime of drawing the boat nearer to the shore and fastening the rope to the pier.

These pantomimes concerning the imaginary boat are best portrayed in "Fighting Against the Chins" (抗 金 兵), "The Intriguers Intrigued" (美 人 計), "The Valiant Fisherman and His Daughter" (打 漁 殺 家), "The Patriotic Beauty, Hsi Shih" (西 施), etc.

XX.   Making Shoe Thread (合 鞋 線) or He Hsieh Sien

The soles of old-fashioned shoes were made of layers of cloth quilted together, a kind of very strong and specially made thread being used for this quilting.   To portray thread-making a "hua-tan" goes through all of the movements of twisting and rolling the imaginary thread. First, she draws out a very long "thread," places the middle of it over an imaginary hook and with one end of it between her teeth and the other between her palms, she rolls it briskly (Illus. 62) so as to twist it tight in one direction.   Exchanging the ends she similarly rolls the other end, and putting the ends together, removes the now twisted thread from the "hook" and holding one end, lets loose the other.   Here the work is completed and she is ready to begin stitching the sole.   This act is portrayed by the actor, playing the maid, Ch'un-lan, in "The Comedy

Illus. 62.   Making Shoe Thread (by Sün Hui-shên)

of Errors" (see synopsis) when she was ordered to make a pair of shoes for Bien Chi, who, of course, could not wear a lady's small shoes.

XXI. To Let Down or Roll Up a Curtain (放 簾 捲 簾) or Fang Lien or Chuan Lien

1. The actor portrays the pantomime of untying the fastening knots of the imaginary rope with which the imaginary curtain is hung and of slowly unrolling the curtain by the following movements: Raise the hands high to the front, looking upward; use the first three fingers of both hands to untie the imaginary knots; then put palms up as if to hold the "rolled curtain"; gradually lower the hands until the imaginary curtain hangs straight to the floor.

2. The actor stoops down to pick up the lower edge of the imaginary curtain, rolls it up until it is high above his head and then fastens it there.

XXII. Drowning in a Well (投 井) or T'ou Tsing

A chair put on one side of the stage may stand for a well. The actor mounts the chair jumps down on the other side and runs quickly off stage.

XXIII. Climbing Over a Wall or a Hill (越 牆 越 嶺) or Yueh Ts'iang or Yueh Lin

A table with a chair at the side is put on the stage (never in centre) to represent a hill or the wall of a building. The actor first throws one end of a rope across the table (received and held by the property-man) and then as if clinging to the rope he mounts the chair and table respectively.

XXIV. Stage Armies (軍 隊) or Chun Tui

Each attendant carrying a large rectangular banner signifies one or two thousand men. These attendants usually enter in fours or in multiples of four.

XXV. Ghosts (鬼) or Kuei

Actors wearing black or red veils or paper tassels represent ghosts.

XXVI. A Patient (病 人) or Ping J'en

When an actor wears a long strip of yellow silk or cloth around his forehead, with its ends hanging down his back, he is considered ill,

XXVII. ENTRANCE AND EXIT (上 場 — 下 場)
OR SHANG CH'ANG—HSIA CH'ANG

On entering the stage the actor must first give the prologue or some line of poetry, or the "tien-chiang-ch'un" tunes (see p. 89), and on exit he must deliver more poetic passages or sing the last sentence in his song.

1. To enter and later to exit through Shang-ch'ang-mên (the entrance curtain) represents that the character returns to the place from whence he has come.

2. To enter and later to exit through Hsia-ch'ang-mên (the exit curtain) means that the character has been summoned by another character on the stage.

3. Characters entering from both curtains show that they come from different directions and happen to meet each other.

4. Characters who exit through both curtains portray that they are going in all directions.

PART III

Classification and Synopses

of Plays

The Classification of Plays

As there has never been any strict rule for the classification of Chinese plays, one may freely classify them according to one's own taste. I venture to classify as follows:

Tragical	Anti-war
Comical	Seasonal or Festival
Tragi-comical	Spectacular
Historical	Superstitious or Mythical
Satirical	Legendary
Sociological	Personal
Romantic	Parallel or Analogous
Ethical	

The Personal Plays are either old plays which have been reconstructed by individual actors or are entirely new plays, written by the present-day literary men and directed or presented by themselves or other artists.

The Parallel or Analogous type are those in which the main plot is almost the same, except:

(a) The leading character is changed, *e.g.* from female star to male or vice versa.

(b) The method of performing is different, *e.g.* in one play singing predominates while in the other acrobatic stunts are prominent.

(c) Only some minor points in the story are different.

A List of Plays Illustrating Each Class:

Tragical

(a) The Final Parting between the King, P'a Wang, and His Favourite (霸 王 別 姬).

(b) The Pass of Chao No. II (武 昭 關).

(c) How the Pass of Boo Was Held (戰 蒲 關).

(d) Hsüeh Yien, the Faithful Concubine (審 頭 刺 湯).

(e) Killing the Tiger General (刺 虎).

(f) The Dream of a Soldier's Wife (春 閨 夢).

(g) Tai Yü at the Burial Mound of Flowers (黛 玉 葬 花).

(h) Offering at the Pagoda (祭 塔).

Comical

(a) A Comedy of Errors (花 田 八 錯).

(b) A Tale of Three Dwarfs (三 矮 奇 聞 即 五 花 洞).

(c) A Nun Seeks Love (思 凡).

(d) The Naughty Maid (春 香 鬧 學).

Tragi-comical

(a) The Royal Monument Pavilion (御 碑 亭).

(b) Snow in June (六 月 雪).

(c) The Tale of the Lute (琵 琶 記).

(d) Loyalty Finds a Way (宇 宙 鋒).

(e) The Lady with a Red-marked Hand (硃 痕 記).

(f) Justice Takes a Holiday but Returns (販 馬 記).

(g) The Romance of Chiang Ts'iu-lien (春 秋 配).

Historical

(a) The Final Parting between the King, P'a Wang, and His Favourite (霸 王 別 姬).

(b) Killing the Tiger General (刺 虎).

(c) Yang Yen-hui Visits His Mother (四 郎 探 母).

(d) The Patriotic Beauty, Hsi Shih (西 施).

(e) Fighting Against the Chins (抗 金 兵).

(f) The Gallant Peace-maker (轅 門 射 戟).

(g) The Strategy of an Unguarded City (空 城 計).

(h) The Intriguers Intrigued (美 人 計).

Satirical

    (*a*) The Valiant Fisherman and His Daughter (打 漁 殺 家).

    (*b*) A Family of Four Virtues (忠孝節義卽三娘教子).

    (*c*) Excessive Taxation Is More Ferocious than the Tiger (荒 山 淚).

Sociological

    (*a*) A Family of Four Virtues (忠孝節義卽三娘教子).

    (*b*) The Romance of Chiang Ts'iu-lien (春 秋 配).

    (*c*) The Royal Monument Pavilion (御 碑 亭).

    (*d*) The Suspicious Slipper (汾 河 灣).

    (*e*) The Significant Sash (香 羅 帶).

    (*f*) Loyalty Finds a Way (宇 宙 鋒).

    (*g*) A Wife's Sacrifice (寶 蓮 燈).

    (*h*) Justice Takes a Holiday but Returns (販 馬 記).

    (*i*) The Lady with a Red-marked Hand (硃 痕 記).

Romantic

    (*a*) The Rainbow Pass (虹 霓 關).

    (*b*) A Comedy of Errors (花 田 八 錯).

    (*c*) The Romance of Chiang Ts'iu-lien (春 秋 配).

    (*d*) A Nun Seeks Love (思 凡).

    (*e*) The Cowherd and the Spinning Maiden (天 河 配).

    (*f*) A Tale of Three Dwarfs (三 矮 奇 聞 卽 五 花 洞).

Ethical

    (*a*) Mu-lan, the Disguised Warrior Maiden (木 蘭 從 軍).

    (*b*) The Patriotic Beauty, Hsi Shih (西 施).

    (*c*) Faithfulness, Fidelity, Purity and Righteousness (節義廉明
        卽 四 進 士).

    (*d*) Snow in June (六 月 雪).

    (*e*) The Lady with a Red-marked Hand (硃 痕 記).

    (*f*) A Family of Four Virtues (忠孝節義卽三娘教子).

    (*g*) An Iron-faced Judge (鍘 美 案).

    (*h*) Hsüeh-yen, the Faithful Concubine (審 頭 刺 湯).

    (*i*) How the Pass of Boo Was Held (戰 蒲 關).

    (*j*) The Reward of Kindness (行 善 得 子 卽 硃 砂 痣).

    (*k*) Killing the Tiger General (刺 虎).

    (*l*) The Royal Monument Pavilion (御 碑 亭).

(*m*) The Dream of a Soldier's Wife (春 閨 夢).

(*n*) Fighting Against the Chins (抗 金 兵).

Anti-war

(*a*) How the Pass of Boo Was Held (戰 蒲 關).

(*b*) The Dream of a Soldier's Wife (春 閨 夢).

(*c*) The Gallant Peace-maker (轅 門 射 戟).

Seasonal or Festival

For the festival of the Seventh Day of the Seventh Moon.

(*a*) The Cowherd and The Spinning Maiden (天 河 配).

For birthday celebrations.

(*b*) Ma-ku Offering Birthday Greetings (麻 姑 獻 壽).

For wedding celebrations.

(*c*) The Reward of Kindness (行 善 得 子 卽 硃 砂 痣).

Spectacular

(*a*) The Patriotic Beauty, Hsi Shih (西 施).

(*b*) Ma-ku Offering Birthday Greetings (麻 姑 獻 壽).

(*c*) The Final Parting between the King, P'a Wang, and His Favourite (霸 王 別 姬).

(*d*) The Golden Mountain Monastery (金 山 寺).

(*e*) Tai Yü at the Burial Mound of Flowers (黛 玉 葬 花).

(*f*) The Dream of a Soldier's Wife (春 閨 夢).

(*g*) The Dream Betrothal (遊 園 驚 夢).

Superstitious or Mythical

(*a*) The Legend of the White Snake Lady (白 蛇 傳).

(*b*) The Cowherd and the Spinning Maiden (天 河 配).

(*c*) A Tale of Three Dwarfs (三 矮 奇 聞 卽 五 花 洞).

(*d*) Ma-ku Offering Birthday Greetings (麻 姑 獻 壽).

(*e*) Spring Romance (牡 丹 亭).

Legendary

(*a*) The Empress' Wrath (罵 殿).

(*b*) History Repeats (蘆 花 河).

(*c*) Love Wins Where Discipline Fails (轅 門 斬 子).

(*d*) A Comedy of Errors (花 田 八 錯).

(*e*) Yang Yen-hui Visits His Mother (四 郎 探 母).

(*f*) A Tale of the Lute (琵 琶 記).

(*g*) Tai Yü at the Burial Mound of Flowers (黛 玉 葬 花).

(*h*) The Suspicious Slipper (汾 河 灣).

(*i*) An Iron-faced Judge (鍘 美 案).

(*j*) Hsüeh-yen, the Faithful Concubine (審 頭 刺 湯).

(*k*) A Family of Four Virtues (忠 孝 節 義 卽 三 娘 教 子).

(*l*) The Red-maned Steed (紅 鬃 烈 馬).

Personal

The personal plays of Mei Lan-fang (梅 蘭 芳)：

(*a*) The Final Parting between the King, P'a Wang, and His Favourite (霸 王 別 姬).

(*b*) Fighting Against the Chins (抗 金 兵).

(*c*) Loyalty Finds a Way (宇 宙 鋒).

(*d*) Tai Yü at the Burial Mound of Flowers (黛 玉 葬 花).

(*e*) The Patriotic Beauty, Hsi Shih (西 施).

(*f*) Mu-lan, the Disguised Warrior Maiden (木 蘭 從 軍).

(*g*) A Family of Four Virtues (忠 孝 節 義 卽 三 娘 教 子).

(*h*) Ma-ku Offering Birthday Greetings (麻 姑 獻 壽).

(*i*) The Romance of Chiang Ts'iu-lien (春 秋 配).

The personal plays of Ch'êng Yen-ts'iu (程 硯 秋)：

(*j*) Liu Yin-ch'un (柳 迎 春).

(*k*) Snow in June (六 月 雪).

(*l*) The Dream of a Soldier's Wife (春 閨 夢).

(*m*) The Lady with a Red-marked Hand (硃 痕 記).

(*n*) Excessive Taxation Is More Ferocious than the Tiger (荒 山 淚).

The personal plays of Sün Hui-shên (荀 慧 生)：

(*o*) The Significant Sash (香 羅 帶).

(*p*) A Comedy of Errors (花 田 八 錯).

The personal plays of Ma Lien-liang (馬 連 良)：

(*q*) Tsŭ-sha Tsing (硃 砂 井 *i.e.* The Great Trial at the Famên Monastery 法 門 寺).

(*r*) I-fêng-hsüeh (一 捧 雪 *i.e.* Hsüeh-yen, the Faithful Concubine 審 頭 刺 湯).

(*s*) Judgment (夜 審 潘 洪).

Parallel or Analogous

(a) { History Repeats (蘆花河).
Love Wins Where Discipline Fails (轅門斬子).

(b) { The Pass of Chao No. I (文昭關).
„ „ „ „ No. II (武昭關).

(c) { The Suspicious Slipper (汾河灣).
The Meeting at Wu Chia Pu (武家坡).

The following plays belong to the *K'un-ch'u* school (崑曲):

Justice Takes a Holiday but Returns (販馬記).
A Tale of the Lute (琵琶記).
The Golden Mountain Monastery (金山寺).
The Meeting at the Fallen Bridge (斷橋).
A Nun Seeks Love (思凡).
Killing the Tiger General (刺虎).
The Naughty Maid (春香鬧學).
The Dream Betrothal (遊園驚夢).
The Dream Comes True (還魂).

Synopses of Plays

Plays on the Chinese stage are not restricted to stories or main plots like the western drama, but by the number of acts. A complete story may comprise a number of "plays" in the Chinese sense of the word, for instance, each part of "The Red-maned Steed" or "The Legend of the White Snake Lady" is considered a play. Therefore, the following fifty synopses are in reality sixty-nine Chinese "plays."

Illus. 63.   The Mistress (by Lee Shih-fang, a boy student of the Peiping Dramatic School) and the Maid (by Mao Shih-lai, another boy student)

PLAY: *A Comedy of Errors*

A COMEDY OF ERRORS

or HUA TIEN PA TSO

（花田八錯）

Liu, a very rich man, had a beautiful daughter, named Yüeh-ying, who preferred to choose her own husband.   (In those days, such choice was made by parents only!) Liu sent Ch'un-lan, the maid, to accompany her to a flower show where she might carry out her purpose (Illus. 63). They happened to pass a shed in which a young scholar, Bien Chi, was trying to make some money by writing poems or prose for people so that he could pay his way to the capital to take the imperial examinations.   Yüeh-ying, falling in love at first sight, sent Ch'un-lan with her fan to say that her mistress wanted him to write a poem on her fan. The clever maid at the same time told him their mission, and asked him to wait for her master's invitation.

When the servant returned with the invited guest, Liu was surprised to find a rough, monster-faced fellow, calling himself Chow Tung, one of Bien's customers.   He said that Bien had been compelled by his friend to go to a birthday celebration, so it must have been the will of Heaven that he was to be the groom.   Liu offered Chow three hundred silver taels (a tael=Sh. $1.40), and begged him to leave, but the latter said that he would return within three days to marry his daughter.

The next morning Yüeh-ying secretly sent Ch'un-lan to see Bien asking him to come disguised as a flower-girl. No sooner had Bien reached Liu's house than Chow arrived to snatch the unwilling bride. As Bien was hiding in Yüeh-ying's bedroom disguised, Chow, in error, roughly put him into the bridal chair. Thinking his daughter had been taken, Liu went to the magistrate to prosecute Chow. Chow therefore, was arrested before he could even enjoy a talk with the supposed maiden.

Consequently, Yu-lan, the only remaining member of the Chow family, was to take care of Bien. She was greatly surprised to discover a young man. Like Yüeh-ying, she fell in love at first sight and gave him two hundred silver taels for his fare to the capital. Having been taken for Bien Chi she was carried to Liu's home, where everything had been made ready for the wedding, because Liu had learned of Bien's substitution and had been expecting him to be brought back in girl's attire. Yu-lan was immediately dressed in the bridegroom's gown and married to the millionaire's daughter. In the bridal chamber, the maidens explained to each other, and each swore to treat the other as sister and marry Bien at the same time.

When Chow got out of prison, he again came to Liu for Yüeh-ying. It happened that a brave monk, Lee Guei, was spending the night with Liu. He volunteered to wear a woman's dress and ride in the chair to Chow's home, where he gave the rascal a hard beating and notified him that because of his evil act his own sister had been lost, and that if he kept on molesting Liu, his own life would be taken.

On the other hand Bien had won the honour of a member of literati and returned to Liu for Yüeh-ying's hand. He was only too glad to find two beautiful brides and a concubine—the maid, Ch'un-lan—waiting for him instead of one would-be wife.

Gramophone Record available:

Tan .... by Chu Chên-ts'iu (朱 釵 秋) .... *Beka*

THE COST OF SAVING
THE MASTER'S SON

or PA NI T'U

(八 義 圖)

T'u, the flattering minister of the King of Tsin, was hostile to the Prime Minister, Chao. He framed some charges which led the King to be suspicious of his faithful minister. Then T'u falsely accused the latter of treason for having attempted to murder the King. Consequently Chao's whole family except Lady Chuang, the King's half-sister, who had married one of Chao's sons, was executed. Before long a son was born to the unfortunate widow.

Hearing of the birth of the Chao baby, T'u insisted that the law must be enforced, so he went into the palace to search for the infant. The lady, however, was too clever to let her precious baby be thus ruthlessly killed. The child had been put under the care of Ch'êng Ing, one of the faithful followers of her husband, whose wife happened to give birth to a son about the same time and was able to nurse both babies.

Failing in the search, T'u offered liberal rewards to anyone who would deliver the baby within ten days. He threatened further that he would kill all the babies in the kingdom of the same age as the Chao child, if the Chao baby was not found.

Therefore, Ch'êng Ing had to consult with Kung-sun, another faithful follower, and as a result of the consultation, they decided on the following plan:

Ch'êng was to sacrifice his only son while Kung-sun at the cost of his life was to pretend to conceal the Chao baby on the Shou-yang Mountain. Then Ch'êng was to report Kung-sun's perfidy. T'u sent men and found the baby. In order to test the friendship between Ch'êng Ing and Kung-sun, T'u ordered the former to thrash the latter. They both played the tragic game so well that everything came out just as they had planned. Kung-sun and Ch'êng's child were executed.

Refusing to accept the reward offered him, Ch'êng requested instead that he and "his son" be allowed to stay in T'u's mansion, for they, he asserted, might be assassinated by some follower of Chao because he had given information concerning the baby's hiding place.

The stupid minister not only sheltered them under his own roof, but adopted the baby and educated him with utmost care. When the fortunate child became a powerful young man, he, following Ch'êng's instructions, killed T'u and his family in revenge.

Gramophone Records available:

Lao-shên ....by	Tan Hsiao-pei	(譚 小 培)...............*Pathé*
„ ....„	Tan Foo-ing	(譚 富 英)............... „
„ ....„	Yu Shu-yen	(余 叔 岩)............*Odeon*
„ ....„	Tan Foo-ing	(譚 富 英)............... „
„ and Ch'in........„	⎧ Tan Foo-ing ⎨ Tan Hsiao-pei ⎩ Kin Shau-shan	(金 少 山)............*Beka*

THE COWHERD AND THE
SPINNING MAIDEN

or T'IEN HÊ P'EI

（天 河 配）

This is a popular play all over China for the festival of the Seventh Day of the Seventh Moon.   The story is as follows:

The dexterous Heavenly Spinning Maiden spun and wove so wonderfully day by day that the beautiful things she made became unrivalled in the heavens.   The Emperor of Heaven was greatly pleased and decided to reward her with a husband.   The choice fell upon the Cowherd, who, though a mortal, had formerly been a fairy in the heavens before he was exiled to the earth because of some misbehaviour.

As a mortal, he was the younger son so his share of the inherited property was in the hands of his elder brother.   The latter's wife had decided to murder him so as to avoid the eventual division of the property.

The elder brother's business trip to a far province offered the sister-in-law an opportunity for action.   She first gave the Cowherd some poisoned noodles, which he threw away after the warning of his fairy cow.   A dog nearby happened to eat the food and died almost instantly. The young man took the attempted murder as an excuse for demanding the division of the property.   The bad woman refused to give him anything, so the Cowherd suggested that if the cow were willing to stay, it should be her property, otherwise, it would be his.   As the woman could not make the cow obey her, she let it leave with the Cowherd.

Illus. 64.   The Spinning Maiden (by Mei Lan-fang)

PLAY: *The Cowherd and the Spinning Maiden*

The fairy cow gave its master everything he wished until one day he wished for a wife. "You have to follow me to the pond where the fairy maidens bathe," said the cow, "and choose a wife for yourself by snatching the dress of the maiden of your choice." Fate had sent the Spinning Maiden (Illus. 64) there. She was so embarrassed when she could not find her dress, that she consented to marry the Cowherd. Overjoyed, the newlyweds forgot all about their duties. This raised the wrath of the Emperor of Heaven who recalled the Spinning Maiden to the heavens to resume her work. The Cowherd hurried after her, but just as he was about to overtake her, the Mother Goddess threw her sash between them. Immediately the sash changed into a broad stream, popularly known as the Milky Way. They wept so broken-heartedly that the Mother Goddess reluctantly granted them a yearly holiday, on the seventh day of the seventh moon, so that they might enjoy a happy rendezvous. The stream, however, was so wide that they were still unable to meet each other. Fortunately, their true love touched the tender hearts of the magpies, who, without being asked, volunteered to build a bridge for them and thus made possible the lovers' meeting on that memorable night.

Gramophone Record available:

Hsiao-shên . . . . by Chiang Miao-hsiang (姜 妙 香) . . . . *Victor*

Illus. 65.   "Tan" (by Ch'êng Yen-ts'iu) and "Hsiao-shên" (by Yu Chên-fei)

PLAY: *The Dream of a Soldier's Wife*

DATE:

110-90 B.C.

THE DREAM OF A SOLDIER'S WIFE

or CH'UN KUEI MÊNG

（春 閨 夢）

The four families, Chao, Chan, Lee and Wong, lived in the same peaceful little village. News came to these peace-lovers that their Emperor, Han Wu-ti, had carried on so many military expeditions against the neighbouring states that conscription was to be enforced all over the country. Soon the order came to the young men of the said families, so Chao had to leave his aged mother and Chan was compelled to put his little son under the sole care of his invalid wife. Since men who went on such expeditions very seldom returned, it seemed that Lee and Wong were bidding their broken-hearted wives eternal farewell.

The play opens with heartrending scenes of parting (Illus. 65) and ends with the climax, the dream scene. Wong and Chao were killed on the battlefield, Chan disappeared, and Lee alone fled home incognito. Wong's bride, Tsing-wan, being left alone on the third day after her wedding, was very much frightened to hear of Chao's death and Chan's disappearance. She did not get any news about her husband so she went to the three neighbours to find whether they had heard of or knew the whereabouts of her husband. Fortunately she failed to get the real truth, so she patiently waited and anxiously inquired whenever she had a chance.

One spring afternoon, while walking in her garden she felt so sleepy that she sat down and leaning against a rock soon fell asleep. She dreamed that her husband returned!

Beginning here, the dream scene takes the form of an operetta. The aesthetic talent of the playwright is best portrayed in this last scene by beautiful songs and dances. The bride begins:

"Why should love-birds be thus separated?
Without you I spend the long days like one in a stupor
Or, like one from whom health has departed.
I have been waiting, waiting for your return;
I sit alone beside the hearth until dawn.
At the time of your departure all flowers were blooming,
But now, the willow is for the second time green.
I look for your letter whenever I hear a noise at the door;
I tremble whenever I hear any news from the front.
Fame and wealth have led man astray,
But to me!
Coarse food and clothing with your company is better than golden
seals (official seal)!"

Gramophone Record available:

Tan ....by Ch'êng Yen-ts'iu (程 硯 秋).................*Victor*

THE EMPRESS' WRATH

or MA TIEN

（罵 殿）

NOTE:—*The origin of this story is doubtful, for it is not recorded in any of the reputable histories. This play was put aside for years, and not given until about ten years ago when Ch'êng Yen-ts'iu （程 硯 秋） came into prominence, winning the honour of being second only to Mei Lan-fang. The song of the Empress' wrath was so well rendered by him that it has become one of the most popular pieces of the "êrh-huang" type.*

Ch'ao K'uang-yin, the first Emperor of the Sung Dynasty (A.D. 960-1277) died leaving a widow and two sons. The throne which should have passed to his son was usurped by the Emperor's brother. Fearing that the young prince, his nephew, might some day become the idol of the people, the wicked uncle so persecuted him that he committed suicide.

The bereaved Empress mother (Illus. 29) was so angry that she openly challenged the usurper to explain why he was not satisfied with the usurpation, but had further indulged himself in killing her son.

Gramophone Records available:

Tan ....by Ch'êng Yen-ts'iu	（程 硯 秋）	..................*Victor*
„ .... „	„	„	..................*Pathé*
„ .... „ Sin Yen-ts'iu	（新 艷 秋）	.... „
Lao-shên .... „ Yen Chü-pêng	（言 菊 朋）	..................*Beka*
„ .... „	„	„	..................*Victor*
„ .... „ Kuan Ta-yüan	（貫 大 元）	.... „
„ and Tan ...... „ ⎰Ch'êng Yen-ts'iu	（程 硯 秋）	
⎱Kuan Ta-yüan	（貫 大 元）	..................*Pathé*

Illus. 66. The Beggar's Costume (by Ch'êng Yen-ts'iu)

PLAY: *Excessive Taxation Is More Ferocious than the Tiger*

EXCESSIVE TAXATION IS MORE
FEROCIOUS THAN THE TIGER

or HUANG SHAN LUI

（荒 山 淚）

Kao Liang-min and his son, Tsong, made their living by gathering medicinal herbs from the mountains. When taxation became still more excessive, they had to go further into the mountains to get more herbs, though they had been warned not to go on account of the tigers.

Once Tsong's wife, Chang Hui-tsu, waited the whole night for her husband and father-in-law, but neither returned. The next morning when she sent her son out to inquire about them, news came that they had been killed by a tiger, for their blood-stained clothes were found near the footprints of the wild beast. Kao's wife, Hui-tsu's mother-in-law, died almost immediately, so she was left alone with her little boy.

At first she tried to raise money by weaving to meet the collectors' extortions, but the better citizens the Kaos proved, the oftener the extortioner came, inventing more forms of taxation to get for himself a fat commission, and for his master, the magistrate, quicker promotion. Until this time the widow had paid whatever was asked, but when she was again ordered to pay another new tax, she answered, "I have paid you all that I have in hand. Both my father-in-law and husband were driven to the tigers by your endless taxation and my mother-in-law died of grief. I do not even have the money to bury her. Please be merciful!" "Don't complain of these deaths, for the loss is on our side,"

171

said the extortioners. "From now on, you need to pay only two-fifths of the head tax you have usually paid. Since you are so wretched, we shall come back after we collect the tax next door."

Afterwards the boy was taken away and sent to labour in the army. The poor woman was so grief-stricken that in delirium she thought she saw her husband running ahead. She followed him until she came to a mountain where she met her neighbour who stopped her with the warning that there were tigers ahead. "I am no longer afraid of the tigers," she exclaimed, "in fact they are most welcome, for now I can die as my husband did. The tax-collectors are much more savage than the tigers." While they were talking, the extortioners were seen coming towards them. The widow, now almost insane, drew out her dagger and attempted to kill them, but she put away the weapon when it was explained to her that they were only doing what they had been told to do (Illus. 66).

Grief and partial insanity eventually caused her to commit suicide and the play ends satirically like this:

A tiger enters, smells the collectors and passes, leaving them unhurt. One of them says, "Most likely we no longer smell like human beings so the beast does not even touch us!"

Gramophone Record available:

Tan ....by Ch'êng Yen-ts'iu (程 硯 秋)...............*Great Wall*

DATE:

ABOUT A.D. 1550

FAITHFULNESS, FIDELITY, PURITY, AND RIGHTEOUSNESS

or SZU TSIN SHIH

（節義廉明卽四進士）

In order to obtain the whole of their inherited property Yao and his wife, Dien-shih, became co-perpetrators in the murder of their brother, Yao Tin-mei. They told Yang, the brother of Yang Soo-tsên, the widow of the deceased, that she should marry again, because she was too young and pretty to remain a widow. The mean brother then sold her a merchant, named Yang Ch'un, who happened to pass the city on his way home to a distant province after collecting his bills.

Yang Ch'un, however, failed to make Yang Soo-tsên his bride. On her telling him of her grief and intention to prosecute the murderers, he not only released her, but adopted her as his sister and promised to help her in the prosecution.

On the way, they met Mao, a fortune-teller—in fact the disguised Inspector-General sent by the Emperor to investigate the conduct of the governors of the various provinces. He volunteered to write the petition for them. They travelled on; some kidnappers finding out that they were strangers took them as an easy prey. The widow was rescued by Wan-shih, the wife of Sung, a competent lawyer. Wan-shih took her to her husband and requested him to accompany her to the magistrate.

173

At first, though Koo, the magistrate, hated and despised lawyers—especially the well-known Sung (for then, lawyers were considered the instigators to litigation, and litigation was the poorest method of settling a dispute)—he dutifully ordered the arrest of Yao, Dien-shih and Yang. When his friend, Dien Lung—the brother of Dien-shih—sent him three hundred taels (a tael=Sh. $1.40) requesting him to dismiss the prosecution, he put Soo-tsên into prison, and gave Sung forty lashes for false accusation.

Fortunately, prior to the above court session, Dien Lung's messengers, sent to bribe Koo, happened to spend the night at Sung's hotel. Overhearing their mission, Sung stole Dien Lung's letter at midnight and obtained a copy of its contents. Now, being thus unjustly punished, Sung started to investigate the whereabouts of the magistrate's superiors. He met Yang Ch'un working at the same task. They soon became friends and agreed to co-operate. Since Yang Ch'un was younger and stronger to bear hardship, it was decided that the latter should present the petition of prosecution, because to discourage litigation the new Inspector-General had proclaimed that whoever dared to file a prosecution to him on the public road, should first suffer forty heavy lashes. How great was his surprise to find the great Inspector-General was none other than the fortune-teller. He pardoned Yang Ch'un the forty lashes and ordered an immediate arrest of all the culprits, including Dien Lung and the magistrate. The copy of Dien Lung's letter was sufficient evidence to convict both the writer and the receiver; however, Dien Lung, who had written the letter under the coercion of his mother, was exempted from punishment, but forever disqualified from holding any public office; Yao, Dien-shih and Koo were executed; Yang, the wicked brother, was sent into exile; Yang Soo-tsên was acquitted; and Sung and Yang Ch'un were duly rewarded.

Gramophone Records available:

Tan ....by Wang You-chun （王 幼 卿）................*Odeon*
Shên .... „ Ma Lien-liang （馬 連 良）................*Pathé*
 „ .... „ „ „ ....*Odeon*

A FAMILY OF FOUR VIRTUES
or SAN NYIANG CHIAO TZǓ

（忠 孝 節 義 即 三 娘 教 子）

Sieh Kuang, leaving a wife, two concubines, and I-ku, a son by the first concubine, at home, went to the capital to take the imperial examinations. The second concubine, Wang Ch'un-ngê, was formerly his servant, so her position was much inferior to that of any other member of the family.

Before reaching the capital, Sieh Kuang was recommended as a medical doctor by a friend to the Emperor, who had fallen sick while leading an army to suppress some border tribes. Sieh Kuang became so very famous in medicine that once while he was away on a visit to the capital, his pupil, in order to attract patients, assumed his master's professional name. Shortly afterwards news of the death of this pupil reached the Sieh family and Sieh Kuang was believed to be dead. Old Sieh Pao, the faithful servant, was sent to bring home his master's corpse. Before his return, the wife and I-ku's mother re-married and took away all Sieh Kuang's property. Wang Ch'un-ngê swore fidelity to her husband and adopted the deserted son. She spun, she wove—in short, she worked hard day and night with Sieh Pao to support and educate the boy (Illus. 67).

Early one afternoon, while weaving (see p. 144, Item XVII) as usual, she was surprised to find I-ku already back from school. The boy not only failed to recite his lessons, but when about to be punished,

Illus. 67. "Wa-wa-shên" (by Lee Yüan-ch'un)

PLAY: *A Family of Four Virtues*

sneered "Please do not beat the son of another woman." She was so brokenhearted that she cut out the unfinished cloth and said she would not make any further effort. Fortunately Sieh Pao intervened and soon made I-ku understand how and why he was adopted by Ch'un-ngê. The boy begged the mother's pardon and declared that henceforth he would be an industrious student.

Not long afterwards, Ch'un-ngê became ill and could not work for days, so I-ku went to his own mother to borrow some money. He returned home empty-handed. Deeply moved he began to study even harder. At sixteen, he passed the imperial examinations and carried home honours to be conferred on his foster mother. When he reached home he found to his great surprise his long-lost father, who was also loaded with honours intended for his wife. The decision was that nobody but Ch'un-ngê was entitled to both the titles and that Sieh Pao was to be chief steward of the Sieh Mansions.

From the loyalty of Sieh Kuang, the fidelity of Ch'un-ngê, the filial piety of I-ku, and the faithfulness of Sieh Pao this play derives its title, "The Family of Four Virtues." The climax is portrayed in the weaving scene, which lasts about forty-five minutes, and most of the parts are sung as in the western opera.

Gramophone Records available:

Tan	.......by	Mei Lan-fang	(梅 蘭 芳)..............*Victor*
„	.... „	Ch'êng Yen-ts'iu	(程 硯 秋).............. „
„	.... „	Shang Hsiao-yuin	(尚 小 雲)............*Beka*
Lao-shên	.... „	Ma Lien-liang	(馬 連 良)........*Odeon*
„	.... „	Wang Yu Ch'un	(王 又 宸).............. „
.,	.... „	Chang Kuei-fun	(張 桂 芬)......*Great China*
Tan and Lao-shên .. „	{ Shang Hsiao-yuin		
	Wang Shau-lou	(王 少 樓)......*Great Wall*	

Illus. 68. Holding the Pheasant Feather (by Mei Lan-fang)

PLAY: *Fighting against the Chins*

FIGHTING AGAINST THE CHINS
or K'ANG CHIN PING

（ 抗 金 兵 ）

During the Sung Dynasty (A.D. 960-1277) the northern borders of China were often invaded by the barbarous tribe, Chin. This tribe became so powerful during the reigns of Huai-tsung and Chin-tsung that they even succeeded in capturing the capital and taking the two emperors as their prisoners. They would have proceeded further south, had they not been driven back by the volunteer generals, Yok Fei and Han Sze-tsong.

The play opens with the Chins' attempt to recapture the northern provinces of China and General Han's preparation to confront the invaders. Liang Hong-yü, Han's wife, proposed first to unite all the neighbouring armies and then advance northward together instead of merely preparing to meet the invasion. A notice was sent to the allied leaders asking them to come together for consultation, but they declined to march forward fearing that they might be defeated by the force of the invaders. Lady Liang pleaded with them in the following words:

"If we choose to wait here, we shall be immediately attacked and if we lose this stronghold and are compelled to retreat further south, we shall lose the whole country north of the River (the Yangtse). Though I am supposed to belong to the weaker sex, my whole family and I prefer fighting even at a big cost to staying here waiting to be

179

attacked and destroyed piecemeal. A broken jade is worth more than an entire tile. Let us choose to be the broken jade, if necessary."

They were stirred by her courage and finally agreed to attack the invaders, electing her their commander-in-chief. She immediately sent Chu Kuei to feign surrender to the Chin leader and to offer him a map with false directions. At the head of this big expedition, the lady so competently planned the strategy of her troops that the Chins were turned back and led into Wang-tien-t'ang, a blind alley.

On learning that Chu Kuei had succeeded in leading the barbarians into the trap, Liang Hong-yü seated herself at the top of Chin Shan, the Golden mountain, in order to give directions with the signal flag. Furthermore, to encourage her soldiers, she herself beat the war drums (Illus. 68) and later took part in the battle. Never before had the Chins met so brave a foe, and never before had the allies fought with such determination. The performance ends with a glorious victory for the immortal heroine's troops.

Gramophone Record available:

Tan . . . . .by Mei Lan-fang (梅 蘭 芳). . . . . *Victor*

THE FINAL PARTING BETWEEN THE KING, P'A WANG, AND HIS FAVOURITE

or P'A WANG PIEH CHI

（霸 王 別 姬）

When the lascivious tyrant Erh-Shih of the Chin Dynasty (221-206 B.C.) ceased to be a competent ruler, all the oppressed took up arms, and heroes, as soon as they had gained some followers, proclaimed themselves kings. From among them Sh'an Yü, the King of Ch'ŭ, and Liu P'ang, the King of Han, emerged as rivals for supremacy. The former was a valiant fighter, straightforward and quick-tempered, but very conceited. It was he who made the remark that if one does not return to his native land after having become prosperous, it is analogous to walking in the dark in one's best attire. His title, P'a Wang, has become a synonym in the Chinese language for a peerless fighter. On the other hand, Liu P'ang, destined to be the founder of the Han Dynasty (202 B.C.—A.D. 220) was very resourceful and crafty.

P'a Wang would have nipped Liu P'ang in the bud had he listened to the advice of his wise counsellor Fan. This opportunity once lost was lost forever. Liu P'ang fled, but after preparing for five years, was again ready to fight at the head of a strong army with the most noted strategist, Han Hsien, as commander-in-chief. P'a Wang was advised to remain quiet and wait until the enemy, coming from afar and burdened with the transportation of supplies, should arrive half exhausted. For some time he listened to his advisors and refused to come out in open battle, but one day Lee Tso-ch'eh, one of Han Hsien's generals,

Illus. 69.   A Posture in the Sword Dance (by Mei Lan-fang).
Meaning of the Posture: Waiting for or prepared to meet an attack.
"Wu-ch'in" (by Kin Shau-shan)

PLAY: *The Final Parting between the King and His Favourite*

simulated surrender to P'a Wang just when reports came that Han Hsien had posted defamatory placards all over the place against him. The play commences here.

Lee made the enraged P'a Wang believe that the time had come for him to lead his army forward to crush his enemy. In spite of the dissuasions of his wise counsellors, even of Lady Yü, P'a Wang ordered his army to advance. Not until he was only forty li (about thirteen miles) from Chiu-li Mountain where Han Hsien had set his fatal trap for P'a Wang, did the latter discover his grave mistake. It was already too late, Lee had absconded. The armies of Han Hsien came out of their ambush and besieged their enemy in overwhelming numbers. P'a Wang would have been killed in the battle, had he not been rescued by his enemy general, Wei Pao, whose family he had once saved.

The survivors were now forced to retreat to Kan-hsia, where Lady Yü tried her best to console her crestfallen king and finally persuaded him to lie down and rest awhile in the camp. She too was filled with sorrow and could not go to sleep. She walked out alone under the moonlight and happened to overhear her soldiers talking about her lord's fate being sealed, and planning to flee back to their native land. Moreover, like the Chinese saying "To snow add frost," she heard songs of her native land sung in her enemy's camp. Frightened, she hastened back to tell her lord. Again they were both deceived by Han Hsien, who had hired men to sing the songs so as to make P'a Wang believe that the majority of his men had surrendered, and to raise the home-sick feeling among the remnant.

Pretending to be cheerful, Lady Yü still endeavoured to strengthen her lord's spirit. With coquettish smiles, she offered him wine and suggested that she dance before him to make him forget his sorrow for the moment (Illus. 69, 71).

However, the approaching war drums soon convinced P'a Wang that he must part with his beloved favourite and march out to confront his enemy. Yet he lingered, because he felt he could not leave her without having first made accommodation for her. Finally he reluctantly told her to go to Liu P'ang as he had heard that the latter loved beauti-ful women. "Leave me, my lord, and charge with your men. Please do not delay your great mission because of a woman," implored the bold Lady. "A loyal minister never serves two sovereigns and a faithful woman refuses to marry a second husband. Lend me your sword, so that I may not stand in your way!" So saying, she snatched her husband's weapon and killed herself.

P'a Wang, once more scourged, went to the battlefield with a new spirit, but being overwhelmingly outnumbered, he barely escaped with his life. He missed his way and was led by a disguised enemy to the bank of the River Wu where he was reminded of his recent crossing at the head of an immense army. Now left alone with only his faithful steed, the humbled P'a Wang felt too embarrassed to return to his native land and therefore committed suicide.

Gramophone Records available:

Tan ....by	Mei Lan-fang	（梅 蘭 芳）	...........*Pathé*
„ .... „	„	„	...........*Beka*
Tan and Ch'in ...... „ {	„ Yang Hsiao-lou	（楊 小 樓）	...........*Great Wall*
Tan and Hsiao-shên .. „ {	Mei Lan-fang Chiang Miao-hsiang	„ （姜 妙 香）	...........*Victor*
Ch'in .... „	Kin Shau-shan	（金 少 山）	...........*Beka*
Lao-shên .... „	Wang Feng-chun	（王 鳳 卿）	...........*Great China*
Ch'ou .... „	Hsiao Ch'ang-hua	（蕭 長 華）	...........*Pathé*

DATE:

A.D. 192-194

THE GALLANT PEACE-MAKER
or YÜAN MÊN SHEH CHI

（轅 門 射 戟）

Liu Pei, destined to be the King of Shu, was just beginning to get a foothold among the warlords in the small city of Hsiao-p'ei, when Yüan Shu, a well-established and prosperous warlord accepted his counsellor's advice to conquer his neighbour states one by one. The first state to be devoured was to be that of Liu Pei, so Yüan sent General Chi to lead an expedition against him and at the same time ordered precious gifts to be presented to Lu Pu, another very able warlord, in order to get his promise not to help Liu.

Hearing of the great expedition, Liu Pei immediately sent messengers to Lu Pu, requesting his help, with the explanation that Yüan would wage war on him, too, if he succeeded in conquering Hsiao-p'ei. Both letters reached Lu about the same time, so he sent invitations to both Yüan and Liu asking them to come to a feast with him.

When Chi arrived and saw Liu Pei, he started to withdraw, but was forced to stay by his host. After the feast, Lu Pu referred to the bad outcome of war-loving men's activities, such as P'a Wang's intrigues (see "The Final Parting between the King and His Favourite"), Han Hsien's, etc. and asked his guests to preserve peace. He then hoisted a "chi" (a lance-like weapon, having a rhomboid-shaped knife at the end and

Chi

185

a curved knife on one of its sides) at a distance of several hundred feet outside his front gate. He said that if he succeeded in shooting through the target, there must be no war. If either of them opposed his peace proposal, he would fight on the side of the one who agreed. Liu Pei was only too glad to agree, while Chi, partly in fear of Lu Pu and partly in the belief that the latter could not succeed, also, though reluctantly, gave his consent.

An arrow was shot and behold, it hit the target! General Chi had to retreat and Lu Pu won the honour of being a gallant peace-maker!

Gramophone Record available:

Hsiao-shên . . . . by Mei Lan-fang (梅 蘭 芳 in jest)[1] . . . . *Odeon*

---

[1] Sometimes, actors play rôles other than their professional ones, to amuse the audience.

DATE:

A.D. 1506-1510

THE GREAT TRIAL AT THE FA-MÊN MONASTERY

or FA MEN SZŬ

（ 法 門 寺 ）

Sun Yü-chiao, the vivacious daughter of a rooster-seller, was embroidering at the front door of her house when a wealthy young man, named Foo Bêng, passed by. The latter was struck by her beauty so he purposely put a jade bracelet in front of her door. She admired the bracelet but she loved the youth more. The incident was noted by a professional match-maker, Liu-shih, who, after Foo's departure, offered herself as their go-between. Yü-chiao was only too glad to have Liu-shih's services and immediately gave her an embroidered shoe to be delivered to Foo as a token of her consent. Liu-shih's son, Piau, a butcher, stole the shoe and was demanding hush money from Foo, when he was detected by a constable, Liu Kung-tao.

Because of his failure in the extortion, the butcher decided to harm Foo. One night he broke into the girl's house and overhearing voices he mistook the persons to be Foo and Yü-chiao. He killed both of them and cut off their heads, which he threw into the courtyard of the constable to get revenge for his friendship with Foo. The constable's hired boy discovered the heads. In great fright, Liu concealed them in the well in his backyard. Fearing the boy might tell the truth, he killed him and also concealed the corpse in the well. Then he shrewdly

sued the boy's father, Sung, a poor unfortunate literary man, for dama-
ges, asserting that the boy had stolen his money and run away. The
incompetent judge, Chao Lien, fined Sung ten taels (a tael=Sh. $1.40).
Since the latter could not pay the fine, his daughter, Sung Ch'iao-chiao,
was kept in custody. It happened that she met Sun Yü-chiao in the
prison and from her discovered that Yü-chiao's lover, Foo, was her
fiance and that they had been unjustly convicted of homicide. The
deceased were Yü-chiao's uncle and aunt, who had been asked to spend
the night with Yü-chiao, because the latter's mother could not return
home that day. The morning after the homicide the court inspector
came to the girl's house and saw the bracelet on Yü-chiao's arm. He
compelled her to disclose the giver's name, for he insisted that a
rooster-seller's daughter could not afford to own or buy such a bracelet.
Consequently, Foo was also arrested. The judge believed the evidence
that Foo and Yü-chiao had killed the victims to facilitate their perpetra-
tion of carnal intercourse, and imposed a death sentence.

Partly to clear the facts about her brother and partly to rescue her
fiance, Sung Ch'iao-chiao volunteered to petition the superiors of the
judge for a new trial. Foo paid the ten taels for her and she was
released. Learning that the Empress-Dowager and her adopted son,
Liu Chin, the Chief Eunuch, were to visit the Fa-mên Monastery to
worship, Sung Ch'iao-chiao waited near-by for days. On their arrival
she shouted aloud pleading for mercy. "Execute her," said the Chief
Eunuch, "Why doesn't she go to the magistrate for justice?" "No,"
remarked the Empress-Dowager, "how can we kill a person while we
are worshipping the gods?"

Therefore, her petition was listened to, and a new trial was granted
with the Chief Eunuch as the Justice of the Imperial Court. Judge Chao
Lien was ordered to arrest all of the real culprits within three days.

From the plaintiff's affidavit, Chao found that the go-between Liu-
shih was involved, so her arrest was ordered. From her, he discovered
that her son had stolen the shoe and kept on trying to extort money
from Foo until Liu Kung-tao's intervention. The butcher's knife proved
the owner's crime and the finding of the heads disclosed Liu kung-tao's
guilt. Instead of one, the poor judge had to deal with two homicide
cases. On the other hand, Sung Ch'iao-chiao was rewarded with ten
silver taels for wrongful detention, and Sun Yü-chao and Foo Bêng

were acquitted. The play ends with the wedding of the three, for then bigamy was allowed in China.

Gramophone Records available:

Lao-shên and Ch'in . . . . by	Tan Foo-ing	(譚 富 英)	*Pathé*
„ „ „ . . . . „	Kin Shau-shan	(金 少 山)	*Beka*
„ „ „ . . . . „	{ Tan Foo-ing		
	Ger Kuei-sien	(裘 桂 仙)	*Odeon*
„ . . . . „	Yen Chü-pêng	(言 菊 朋)	„
„ . . . . „	Wang Shau-lou	(王 少 樓)	*Great China*
Ch'in and Ch'ou . . . . „	{ Kin Shau-shan		
	Ma Foo-lok	(馬 富 祿)	*Beka*
„ „ „ . . . . „	{ Hê Shou-ch'ên	(郝 壽 臣)	
	Ju Foo-hui	(茹 富 蕙)	*Great Wall*
Ch'in . . . . „	Hê Shou-ch'ên	. . . .	*Victor*

The play opens with the announcement of the coming of General Sieh Tin-shan into the presence of his wife, Fan Lee-hwa, who is a general of even greater prowess.

General Sieh tells his wife that he has heard that she intends to execute their adopted son, because, contrary to military law, the latter had married one of the daughters of an enemy at Loo-Hwa Hê, where he had been sent to lead the battle.

The mother general at first is deaf to the entreaties of her husband, arguing that she is determined to carry out the order and maintain her reputation for discipline.

When the husband reminds her that they had been married under similar circumstances she repents and forgives her son on the condition that in the future his military exploits shall redeem his error.

Gramophone Records available:

Tan . . . . by	Ch'êng Yü-tsin	（程 玉 菁）	. . . . *Beka*
Tan and Shên . . . . „	⌠ Ch'êng Yen-ts'iu ⌡ Kwok Ts'ong-heng	（程 硯 秋） （郭 仲 衡）	. . . . *Pathé*
„ „ „ „	⌠ Tu Lee-yuin ⌡ Kwok Ts'ong-heng	（杜 麗 雲）	. . . . *Great Wal*

HOW THE PASS OF P'U WAS HELD

or CHAN P'U KWAN

（戰 蒲 關）

A big battle was fought and Wang Pa, defeated on account of lack of men and supplies, was forced to retreat to hold the Pass of P'u. For months he had been besieged by overwhelmingly superior forces. Both men and supplies decreased day by day until one night the hungry survivors became mutinous. Wang was compelled to find out some way to satisfy his men or the city would be destroyed.

He had an idea, though it was a heart-breaking one! He planned to kill his beloved concubine, Hsu Yen-tsêng, so that he might give her body to feed his soldiers. He had to withhold his sword for the virtuous lady was found praying in the back garden. He overheard her praying for the arrival of reinforcements so that her people's trouble might be averted, for the peace of her husband and for the birth of a son to her mistress, Wang's wife. She was too good to be so savagely murdered!

Liu Tsong, Wang's faithful servant, learned of his master's plan and volunteered to die in her stead, but, because of Liu's low status, Wang deemed his death insufficient to move his men, so he begged him to kill the concubine for him. Liu loitered but finally went inside where he found Yen-tsêng reading by candle-light. She was so excited and worried that she had not been able to go to sleep. She was astonished to see Liu come at such a late hour, and became very much puzzled when Liu told her that his master wanted to borrow some food from her. Since she had given her husband everything she possessed, she could not understand his request. Not until she espied the sword Liu held behind him, did she realize that she was to give him her own body. She boldly accepted the sword and killed herself. Then Liu also killed himself to assist his master in the completion of his plan.

The result was that the whole army was deeply touched. They stood with their leader as one man and eventually succeeded in holding the Pass until reinforcements came to their aid.

Gramophone Records available:

Tan ....by Mei Lan-fang	（梅 蘭 芳）	...............*Great Wall*
„ .... „ Ch'êng Yen-ts'iu	（程 硯 秋）	.... „ *China*
„ .... „ Shang Hsiao-yuin	（尚 小 雲）	...............*Victor*
„ .... „ „	„	...............*Odeon*
Lao-shên .... „ Yen Chü-p'êng	（言 菊 朋）	.... „

HSÜEH-YEN, THE FAITHFUL
CONCUBINE
or SHEN T'OU T'ZŬ T'ANG

（審 頭 刺 湯）

During the decline of the Ming Dynasty (A.D. 1368-1644) the Emperor reigned but did not govern, for the real ruler had long been the powerful, unscrupulous Prime Minister, Yen Sung. Whenever he set his mind on getting an object, he would obtain it regardless of the means employed. He forgave no one who dared to disobey him.

When he heard that Mê Huai-ku owned a jade cup, named "I-fêng-hsüeh," a priceless curio, he sent him word that he wanted to borrow it. A skilful jeweller offered to copy it and Mê was only too glad to listen to his advice and to send the imitation to Yen. The cup was so artfully made that the covetous Prime Minister was very pleased to receive it.

T'ang Ch'in, however, one of Yen's followers, whom Mê once rescued, knew the peculiar features of the cup. He disclosed Mê's deception to his present master, not because of devotion to him, but on account of his desire to win Hsüen-yen, the beautiful concubine of his benefactor. Mê was thrown into prison on a false charge of murder. Yen ordered the judge to impose a death sentence on the innocent man.

Mê Chêng, whose appearance bore a close resemblance to that of his unfortunate master, Mê Huai-ku, offered to be executed in his place. The judge, being a friend of Mê and knowing his innocence, agreed to the proposal and the loyal servant was decapitated.

193

Illus. 70· Aside: 1—"Wên-ch'ou" (by Hsiao Ch'ang-hua); 2—"Tan"
(by Mei Lan-fang)

PLAY: *Hsüeh-yen, the Faithful Concubine*

The Prime Minister's appointment of T'ang Ch'in to test the identity of the owner of the decapitated head (the head is represented by a round bundle wrapped in red cloth) gave the latter the chance to satisfy his desire. Lu Pin, the judge, realized that unless the concubine consented to marry T'ang, Mê's life was still in danger, so the clever judge suggested the situation to her by showing her the word "assassinate," which he wrote on his fan, and by intimating to her that she feign to marry T'ang. Then he purposely left the latter alone with the concubine (Illus. 70), who beguilingly said, "Since the first time I met you on the West Lake, I've loved you, but we have been robbed of the chance even to meet each other! Fortunately I am a widow now!"

T'ang identified the head as being that of Mê. Therefore, the concubine consented to marry him immediately. On the wedding night the groom could not resist the repeated offerings of wine by the bride so that he became helplessly intoxicated. Then the loyal but avenging woman drew his sword (Illus. 36) and drove it through the breast of the ungrateful monster.

Fearing that she might be questioned or might in some way reveal the truth that Judge Lu Pin was in a way involved in this murder, she committed suicide.

Gramophone Records available:

Tan ....by	Mei Lan-fang	(梅 蘭 芳)...............*Beka*
,, ... ,,	Sün Hui-shên	(荀 慧 生)...............*Odeon*
,, ... ,,	Yuln Yen-lisla	(雲 艷 霞)...............*Viotor*
Tan and Ch'ou ...... ,,	⎰ Mei Lan-fang ⎱ Hsiao Ch'ang-hua	(蕭 長 華)...............*Victor*
Shên .... ,,	Ma Lien-liang	(馬 連 良)...............*Pathé*
,, ... ,,	,,	,, ...*Odeon*
Ch'ou .... ,,	Hsiao Ch'ang-hua	...............*Pathé*

Illus. 71.   A Posture in the Sword Dance: 1—"Wu-ch'in" (by Kin Shau-shan)
2—"Tan"; The Fencing Hand (by Mei Lan-fang)

PLAY: *The Final Parting between the King and His Favourite*

THE INTRIGUERS INTRIGUED

or MAI JÊN CHI

（美 人 計）

or KAN LU SZU

（甘 露 寺）

During the period of the Three Kingdoms (A.D. 190-280) there lived in the Kingdom of Wu the princess, Sun Shang-hsiang, the youngest sister of the King, Sun Ch'üan. She was not only beautiful, but also well educated both in literature and military tactics. Her mother was so proud of her that she set up severe qualifications for those who ventured to sue for her hand.

Sun Ch'üan and his admiral, Chou Yü, intrigued to capture Liu Pei, the ruler of the Kingdom of Shu. Pretending that the King Sun Ch'üan was to give Liu Pei his sister's hand, Chou Yü invited Liu Pei to come across the boundary river to get married. Knowing that it was an insincere proposal, Chu-kê Liang, Liu Pei's strategist, decided to play a trick on the intriguers. He therefore advised Liu Pei to accept the invitation with only one general, Chao Yuin, accompanying him. Of course, he gave both of them instructions how to meet the various situations on their arrival at Wu.

As soon as Liu Pei and Chao Yuin crossed the river, they went to see the Honourable Chiao Hsüan, the father-in-law of Chou Yü, to solicit his assistance. The latter, having received many costly gifts from Liu Pei, gave him, in return, a kind of drug to dye his gray beard so as to make him look like a young man. The next day, the Honourable Chiao Hsûan went to see the old mother and told her of her son's intrigue. Moreover, he praised Liu Pei so highly that she was finally persuaded to summon him to Kan Lu Szŭ (a monastery) to be examined whether or not he was qualified to be the husband of the fair princess. The result was that he was chosen and the wedding took place almost immediately.

The bride was so lovely that the groom even forgot to go home. The faithful general, Chao Yuin, following Chu-kê Liang's instructions, delivered a false message to his master that the army of the Kingdom of Wei had been mobilized and was about to attack Chingshow (one of the most important cities of Shu). He also warned him that his further stay in Wu would surely result in the loss of that city. Hesitatingly he told the Princess of his country's trouble. To his great surprise, the dutiful bride consented to follow him home. When she went to bid her mother farewell, the thoughtful old Lady, fearing that her son (the King) might hinder their departure, gave her the "Shang Fang" sword (the possessor of which was considered the representative of the Sovereign) to protect them.

On the way, Sun Ch'üan's men did try to arrest Liu Pei and Chao Yuin, but the sword of the Princess "escorted" them to the bank of the river in safety, where Chang Fei, Liu Pei's brother by adoption, sent by Chu-kê Liang, was more than ready to welcome them home.

Gramophone Records available:

Lao-shên .... by Ma Lien-liang （馬連良）............... *Beka*
    „ .... „ Wang Shau-lou（王少樓）............... *Great Wal.*
    „ .... „ Kuan Ta-yüan（貫大元）............... *Victor*
Lao-tan .... „ Lee Too-ku'ei （李多奎）................ *Beka*

AN IRON-FACED JUDGE

or TSE MI AN

(鍘 美 案)

Chen, a poor scholar, had a beautiful and diligent wife, named Shian-lien, and two sons. The woman worked day and night to make money, not only to relieve Chen of his family burden but to finance his trip to the capital for the imperial examinations. She proved to be a success as a business woman, but she was not so fortunate as a wife, for Chen, after having passed all the examinations was only too glad to marry the Emperor's sister. Royal luxuries made him forget his hard-working benefactress, Shian-lien.

In the meantime the anxious family waited and waited, until one day word of Chen's marriage into the royal family reached the home town. Overhearing the news, Shian-lien decided to work her way to the capital so that her two children might be properly benefited by their father's present position, even if her husband had decided to abandon her.

For months the three struggled on until at last they found themselves before Chen's stately palace. At first they were not recognized and were driven out. Later, the helpless woman and children were placed in the back garden by one of Chen's servants, who took pity on them. Chen, to prevent further disturbance, sent one Han-chi to murder them. Fortunately a kind-hearted maid heard of the plan and secretly slipped to the garden to warn Shian-lien to escape. Suspecting that the unknown maid was sent by her husband to get them out of his way, the latter refused to leave. Not until the maid killed herself before her to avoid her master's punishment for disclosing the plot, did Shian-lien and the children start to escape. They were soon overtaken, however, by Han-chi at a deserted temple.

The pitiful group knelt before Han, pleading for mercy and explaining to him their relation to his master. Han was touched and set them free, but he paid the penalty for disobeying his master's orders by killing himself with the sabre which Chen had given him to murder his wife and children.

Shian-lien, thus oppressed, was forced to seek justice from P'ao, nicknamed the Iron-faced Judge, who dared to execute justice, even against the Emperor's nearest relatives or favourites.

In order to prevent any obstacle to the arrest of Chen, as the latter was living in the Princes' palace, P'ao dispatched his man, Wang, to pretend to be the murderer of Han-chi, Chen's servant. Wang succeeded in enticing Chen to come to P'ao for prosecution. Then the prosecutor instead of the prosecuted was immediately put to trial. Chen insisted that he did not know the woman (Shian-lien) and her children, even when the latter showed him the sabre bearing his name and fitting exactly the case hanging on the belt of Han-chi. Moreover, Chen defied P'ao and maintained that the Emperor alone should decide the case. The Iron-faced Judge answered coldly, "Since the evidence is sufficient, you are no longer a member of the royal family, but a convicted criminal in the eyes of the law. Your very noble position shall not extenuate, but aggravate your punishment."

The Princess and the Empress Dowager both came to the rescue but P'ao declared, "Law is law; the judicial decision shall not be interfered with by outside influence. As the Emperor has given me three methods of execution for the three classes of society, the nobles, the middle class and the low class, this man shall not be an exception!" Therefore, Chen was eventually beheaded.

Gramophone Record available:

Ch'in . . . . by Kin Shau-shan (金少山) . . . . *Pathè*

JUDGMENT

or YEH SHÊN P'AN HUNG

（夜 審 潘 洪）

P'an Hung, the father of the Emperor's favourite, so hated the righteous general Yang Chi-yeh and his sons that he sent them to the most dangerous posts with a small number of men and very poor equipment. Naturally they were easily wiped out by the overwhelming enemy. Yang Yen-chao, the sixth son, was the only one who returned to prosecute P'an for murder. The judge, bribed by the favourite, did not admit the proper evidence against the perpetrator, which act aroused the wrath of the Emperor's uncle, who killed the judge with his All-powerful Club, a reprimanding weapon inherited from the founder Emperor. In due time, he proceeded to compel the Emperor to agree to summon Judge Kou-Tsen, noted for being an upright man, to try the case. The favourite also tried to bribe the second judge, who cleverly accepted the liberal gift and sent it to the royal uncle without opening it.

Since it was the custom that no matter how relevant the evidence was to the facts, a confession from the criminal was required and since the shrewd prisoner refused to speak, Judge Kou Tsen could not proceed satisfactorily.

One stormy night, P'an was awakened by Ox-head and Horse-face (believed to be the attendants of the King of Death and so named because of their peculiar physical features. It was their duty to arrest the souls of wicked men to be tried in the ghost court where nothing could be concealed). They took him—only half-awake—out into the storm with such hasty steps that old P'an was made to believe that they were supernatural. They dragged him on and on until they came to a queer structure somewhat like a state court building. The frightened and exhausted prisoner was then thrown before the solemn Judge of the Dead, who conducted the trial so well that a willing confession was written and signed. No opportunity was left for the Emperor to be partial to his favourite's father. He could do nothing but regretfully sign the mandate of P'an's execution.

Gramophone Records available:

Lao-shên ....by	Ma Lien-liang	(馬 連 良)...............	*Victor*
,, ... ,,	,,	,, ...	*Beka*
,, ... ,,	Yen Chü-pêng	(言 菊 朋)...............	,,
Ch'in .... ,,	Kin Shau-shan	(金 少 山)...............	*Great Wall*
,, ... ,,	Hê Shou-ch'ên	(郝 壽 臣)...............	*Beka*
,, ... ,,	,,	,, ...	*Victor*

Lee Kuei-chih, the wife of the magistrate of the city of Pao was alone one night in her home. At a late hour she was disturbed in her inner apartment by hearing the pitiful groans of an old man. (The transporting of the groans by the wind-gods is portrayed on stage by two actors, standing on chairs, furling and unfurling flags so as to show that the sound is caught in the flag and sent over the walls into the inner apartments.) She soon discovered that the groans came from a tortured prisoner, who was unable to meet the jailor's extortion. She sent for him, and great was her surprise when she found that he was her father, Lee Chi, who had been thrown into prison through the intrigue of her step-mother and the latter's paramour.

Some years before, when Lee Chi was away selling horses, the step-mother had driven out Kuei-chih and her younger brother, Pao-t'ung. On Lee Chi's return the step-mother had told him that both of the children had died of illness. Distrusting his wife, Lee Chi compelled the maid-servant to tell the truth about what had happened and she, in great fear of her mistress, committed suicide. Lee Chi was prosecuted for rape and for eventually causing the death of the girl.

In the meantime the children had wandered into the forest and, seeing a tiger, lost each other in their effort to escape. Kuei-chih was fortunately adopted by a rich man, and was later married to Chao Ch'ung, the magistrate.

On hearing from her father the story of his unfair trial, Kuei-chih immediately asked her husband for help. He persuaded her to disguise herself as his attendant and to go with him to petition the new viceroy for a second trial. It happened that the latter was her brother, Pao-t'ung, who, having failed in his search for his sister, had worked his way up to the capital, passed the imperial examinations and, being very clever, had been promoted to a viceroyship.

All the wicked were duly punished and a very happy reunion ends the play.

Gramophone Records available:

Tan ....by	Sün Hui-shên	(荀慧生)............*Great Wall*
Tan and Shên ..... „	{ Mei Lan-fang { Chiang Miao-shang	(梅蘭芳) (姜妙香)..............*Victor*
„ „ „ ..... „	{ Koo Ch'uen-cha { Chu Ch'uen-min	(顧傳玠) (朱傳茗)..............*Beka*

KILLING THE TIGER GENERAL

or T'ZU HU

（刺 虎）

When Emperor Ch'ung-chêng, the last sovereign of the Ming Dynasty (A.D. 1368-1644), hanged himself on Mei Shan (literally, coal hill), in the centre of the capital, Peking, when the city fell into the hands of Lee, the rebel leader, one of his maids, Fei Chêng-ngê, swore vengeance upon the rebels for the death of her royal Master. She therefore impersonated the princess in order to attract the attention of the rebel leader.

As a reward to his favourite warrior, known as the dauntless "Tiger" general, Lee gave him the disguised princess instead of making her his own bride. Though Shêng-ngê felt somewhat disappointed at the lost opportunity, she consoled herself with the thought of being given the chance to kill the "Tiger."

She put on her best apparel, prepared good wine and on the arrival of the groom, entertained him in such a splendid manner that the "Tiger" was immediately infatuated. He was greatly pleased to hear her praises and was helpless under her charm (Illus. 72). Wine, poured by her dainty hands, was too sweet to be rejected, so cup after cup was drunk until the victim was helplessly intoxicated. She dismissed the maid-servants saying that henceforth she alone would serve him. Then she asked the general to let her take off his armour and put away his sword as he had a seriously-wounded arm. Besides, she said, it would seem

Illus. 72. 1—The Resting Sleeves (the Maids on the sides by Yao Yü-fu and
Chu Kuei-fang); 2—The Repulsing Sleeve ("Tan" by Mei Lan-fang);
3—"Wu-ch'in" (by Liu Lien-yung)

PLAY: *Killing the Tiger General*

very improper and unlucky for the groom to wear man-killing weapons on his wedding night.

Finally, with the "Tiger" put to bed like a pet lamb, she blew out the candles (see p. 25, Item 14) and waited until he was sound asleep (Illus. 73). Then she drew forth her dagger and plunged it quickly into his bosom. Fiercely they struggled in the dark, until she recollected the place where she had put the "Tiger's" sword, and with it she now stabbed its owner. When she made her identity known to the ignorant maidservants, who accused her of cold blooded murder, she felt so disappointed that she committed suicide, grieving that she did not have the opportunity to kill the rebel leader.

Gramophone Records available:

Tan	by Mei Lan-fang	(梅 蘭 芳)	*Victor*
Tan and Ch'in	„ { Shang Hsing-wu	(項 馨 吾)	
	Hsu Moo-yien	(徐 摹 煙)	*Odeon*
	(dramatic amateurs)		

Illus. 73. "Chang-tzŭ"; "Wu-ch'in" (by Liu Lien-yung);
"Tan" (by Mei Lan-fang); "Têng Tso"

PLAY: *Killing the Tiger General*

THE LADY WITH A
RED-MARKED HAND
or CHU HÊN CHI

（牧 羊 卷 即 硃 痕 記）

On account of his uncle's age and delicate health, Chu Ch'un-têng went to the army in his place, leaving his aged mother to the care of his beautiful and faithful wife, Chao Chin-t'ang. The uncle's wife, Sung-shih, intending to rob Ch'un-têng of his property and to enable her nephew, Sung Ch'êng, to marry Chao Chin-t'ang, sent Sung Ch'êng to murder Ch'un-têng on his way to join the army. Fortunately, a hunter appeared on the scene and saved Ch'un-têng's life.

Sung then spread the news that Ch'un-têng had been killed on the battlefield. Grief hastened the death of the old, sickly uncle and the entire family property fell into Sung-shih's hands. She tried to compel Chin-t'ang to agree to marry her nephew. On her refusal she persecuted her and her mother-in-law and made them do all kinds of hard tasks. To relieve the old mother, Chin-t'ang always did double work. They were forced to grind flour during the daytime, and even on snowy or stormy nights were made to stay outdoors to watch over the sheep. Still Sung-shih was dissatisfied, so she drove them from home. It was a time of famine, and the two wretched women had to beg for a living. They wandered from place to place until one day they happened to pass their ancestral tombs where they saw a grand pavilion had been put up. Memorial services for the dead were to be conducted there. They were surprised!

209

Free meals were being distributed to the poor, but they were already too late to obtain any food that time. They had to wait for the next meal. Being desperately hungry, Chao Chin-t'ang knelt before the servants begging for some food, even some remnants for her mother-in-law only. One man, touched by her filial piety, gave her some rice left over by his master, the Earl, who was none other than Chu Ch'un-têng, now a great war hero, and had come back to share his honours with his mother and wife. Being told by Sung-shih that they were dead, the Earl was so disappointed that he decided to give up his official career, stay in his pavilion and give alms to the poor in memory of his beloved ones.

Chin-t'ang handed the remnant of rice to the mother, who being over-excited at the daughter's good heart, dropped the bowl and broke it. The servant's scolding was overheard by the Earl, who immediately sent for the beggars to find out whether the servant had maltreated them. The mother was afraid to see such a great man, so Chin-t'ang went in alone. The red mark on the lady's hand proved to the Earl that she was none other than his missing wife and he was told that the old beggar outside was his dear mother, for whom he had mourned so deeply.

Afraid of the consequences of what she had done, Sung-shih jumped into a well (see p. 147, Item XXII) nearby.

The play ends with the happy re-union.

Gramophone Records available:

Lao-tan and Chin-i ...... by	Ch'êng Yen-ts'iu	(程 硯 秋) .... *Great China*
	Wên Liang-ch'ên	(文 亮 臣) .... „
„ „ „ .... „	Shang Hsiao-yuin	(尙 小 雲) .... *Great Wall*
	Lee Too Ku'ei	(李 多 奎) .... *Beka*
Lao-shên .... „	Tan Hsiao-pei	(譚 小 培) .... „
„ .... „	Yen Chü-pêng	(言 菊 朋) .... *Victor*
„ .... „	Kuan Ta-yüan	(貫 大 元) .... *Great China*

Ming, a scholar, left his brother's home for the capital to take the imperial examinations. On his return, he learned that his brother had died suddenly. His widowed sister-in-law was not only light-hearted but tried repeatedly to flirt with him. This aroused his suspicion and he decided to investigate the real cause of his brother's death. The widow was quite willing to give up Hou, her present paramour for Ming, but the latter's refusal compelled her to plan his death to avoid being discovered in her crime with Hou. Hou murdered his wife, hid her head, put the corpse before Ming's door and concealed the widow at his home. Then he prosecuted Ming for rape of his brother's widow and murder on the victim's resistance.

The incompetent judge threw Ming into prison, and by unbearable tortures made him sign an untrue confession. His faithful servant, Ma-I, went to the magistrate to testify to his master's innocence. The judge tested him, saying, "If you want to save your master, find the missing head and bring it to me." The simple-minded servant tried to "borrow" his only daughter's head to save his master, but he could hardly raise his knife against the innocent maiden. She, however, upon learning of her father's aim, killed herself. The head was taken to the magistrate who at once discerned that the head was too fresh to be the missing one. The broken-hearted father was forced to tell the truth. The merciless judge convicted Ming of murder, regardless of the evidence Ma offered.

Ma then went to the capital to try to effect a new trial, but not until he was bold enough to suffer the ordeal of throwing himself upon a board of sharp nails did the Prime Minister grant a new trial. A swift messenger was sent to postpone the execution of the death sentence. It happened that the critical night was extraordinarily long. The sentinels went nine rounds instead of the usual five. As the convicted man was not to be executed until dawn, the messenger was able to reach his destination in time.

Gramophone Record available:

Lao-shên ....by Kao Chun-ku'ei (高 燮 奎)................*Pathé*

THE LEGEND OF THE WHITE SNAKE LADY
or PÊ SHEN CH'ÜAN
(白 蛇 傳)

NOTE:—*Parts I-II are sung to the southern melody, "Kun-ch'u," accompanied by the flute, but Parts III-IV are usually given in "P'i-huang" music, with the accompaniment of the "hu-ch'in" (Chinese violin).*

PART I.   THE GOLDEN MOUNTAIN MONASTERY
or KIN SHAN SZU (金 山 寺)

A White Snake, by years of consecration, had been transformed into a semi-fairy in the form of a beautiful lady.   She was ordered by the Emperor of Heaven to descend to earth to serve Hsü Sien, a poor scholar in Hangchow, in compensation for his rescuing her from a beggar's hand.   The kind youth had bought the little White Snake and compassionately set it free.

On her way down she met a Blue Snake, also a semi-fairy lady, but inferior in rank and virtue.   They became friends and decided to go to earth together.   Through the help of the Blue Snake, she succeeded in marrying her saviour.   She and the Blue Snake, who now posed as her maidservant, made the husband prosperous and they lived happily until one day a monk, named Fa-hai, told Hsü Sien that his wife and maid were not mortals but transformed snakes and that he would be poisoned by them if he continued to live with them.   He was greatly frightened and so he hid himself in the temple of Fa-hai, the Golden Mountain Monastery.

The White Snake Lady finally grew impatient waiting for her husband, so she went to the monastery to find him (Illus. 74).   The

213

Illus. 74.   Miss Hsüeh Yen-ch'in in the Rôle of the White Snake Lady

PLAY: *The Legend of the White Snake Lady*

monk refused even to let her see him. She argued and pleaded, but in vain. In desperation she sought help from her adopted brother, the Spirit of Black Fish, who subsequently brought on a terrible tempest and flooded the whole district, threatening the monk that if he refused to yield, he would sweep away the whole monastery. Fa-hai threw his fairy gown at the rising flood and made it subside at once, but not before the villages were deluged and many lives were lost. Therefore, the Snake Lady was sentenced to everlasting imprisonment under the Lui-fung Pagoda on the West Lake in Hangchow. (Much to the joy of her sympathizers, this pagoda crumbled down a few years ago, thereby liberating the White Snake Lady.)

Another version of the play, however, says that when the merciless monk threw the fatal "Spirit-captivating Urn" at the Lady, she was rescued by the Star of Literature, who came to protect her unborn child, destined to be the head of the literati of that day.

PART II. THE MEETING AT THE FALLEN BRIDGE

or TUAN CH'AO (斷 橋)

Disappointed by the incident at the Golden Mountain Monastery, the White Snake Lady started to go back to Hangchow with the Blue Snake maid. Approaching the city, she felt so tired and sick that she had to stop by the roadside, where she saw a man run suddenly as if to avoid them. It was the heartless husband! They struggled on after him and finally overtook him at the Fallen Bridge on the West Lake. The maid was so angry that she started to kill him, but the Lady stood between them begging her to give him one more chance to explain. He of course put all the blame on the monk and knelt before the Lady as if in repentance, saying that he was grieved to have seen her suffer and that he had run away because of embarrassment.

Though the maid did not believe one single word and advised the mistress to leave him forever, yet the devoted wife loved her husband and said that she would follow him to his sister's home nearby. The play ends here with a temporary reconciliation, for soon after the baby came, Hsü Sien threw the fatal urn at his wife, which action immediately transformed her into a snake again.

PART III. THE ARREST OF THE WHITE SNAKE LADY
or HÔ PO (合 鉢)

Not long after the White Snake Lady arrived at the home of her husband's sister, she gave birth to a son. During the month of confinement, she could not use her magic power to foresee future events and was unable to guess what her husband was planning. She was, however, a very strong and capable mother, and prepared for her son's needs ten years in advance.

When the child was one month old the heartless husband threw the "Spirit-captivating Urn" at her. She was again transformed into a white snake. Almost immediately the cruel monk, Fa-hai, came to take her away and imprisoned her in the Lui-fung Pagoda. Hsü Sien, repenting of having so maltreated his wife, begged the monk to have mercy on her and the motherless baby, but it was too late. In great remorse Hsü Sien became a monk and devoted himself to the gods for the redemption of his soul.

PART IV.   OFFERING AT THE PAGODA or TSI T'A (祭 塔)

At the time when the poor mother began her sentence of everlasting imprisonment under the Lui-fung Pagoda, her son, Shih-lin, was only one month old. He was reared by his paternal aunt.

In boyhood, he was often insulted by his schoolmates who said that his mother was a snake, and that he therefore was only partly human. He kept on asking his aunt about his parents until he was promised that he would be told the whole truth when he had won the honour of being the head of the literati.

The boy studied hard and at sixteen actually fulfilled his aunt's condition. After learning that his mother was imprisoned in the pagoda, he immediately secured a special mandate from the Emperor ordering the local officials to prepare an elaborate offering to be sent to the White Snake Lady at the pagoda and allowing the son, Shih-lin, to attend the ceremony.

The play portrays the pathetic meeting of the Lady and her son. The actor who takes the female rôle must have a voice not only good but strong, for the song of the Lady's life should be sung to the strenuous "fan-êrh-huang" tune for about thirty minutes, without pause. In recent years this play has been very rarely performed on the Chinese stage, because the majority of actors prefer not to undertake this task.

Gramophone Records available:

Tan ....by Mei Lan-fang   (梅 蘭 芳)..................*Pathé*
  „ .... „ Shang Hsiao-yuin   (尙 小 雲)..................*Odeon*
  „ .... „ Yuin Yen-hsia   (雲 艷 霞)..................*Victor*

Illus. 75. The Unfounded Suspicion ("Tan," by Mei Lan-fang; "Lao-shèn," by Wang Shau-t'ing)

PLAY: *The Suspicious Slipper*

LIU YING-CH'UN
or THE SUSPICIOUS SLIPPER
(柳 迎 春)
or FEN HÊ WAN
(汾 河 灣)

NOTE:—*"Liu Ying-ch'un," performed only by Ch'êng Yen-ts'iu* (程 硯 秋), *is the whole story, whereas "The Suspicious Slipper" depicts merely the latter part of the lady's life.*

After a night of heavy snow, Liu Ying-ch'un, the pretty daughter of a rich aristocratic family, climbed the high tower (p. 27, Item 20) in her father's garden to enjoy the beautiful view of the silvery world. She saw a manly youth shivering while working in the cold. Taking pity on him, she threw down a coat and went in without letting him know the identity of the donor. The young man, Sieh-li, who was one of her father's workmen, had to thank heaven for the providential gift.

The stern, conservative father was surprised to see the splendid coat, so he asked the young man where it came from. Dissatisfied with the answer, the old man began to suspect his daughter's chastity. His wrath grew so great that he ordered the maiden to be put to death. The kind mother secretly let her escape through the back door and ordered her old nurse to accompany her. At a deserted temple outside the city, they happened to meet the handsome Sieh-li. The nurse, knowing at first sight that the youth was not an ordinary working man and would someday be great if he were given a chance, became their matchmaker. They were married. Unable to rent a house they had to live in a "yao," *i.e.* a sort of cave dug out of the hillside.

Sieh-li, failing to find a good position at home, was forced to try his fortune in the army. The play ("The Suspicious Slipper") opens when the faithful wife has waited patiently for eighteen years together

219

with her seventeen-year-old boy, Sieh Tin-shan, born seven months after her husband's departure. Every morning she sends her son to Fên Hê Wan to fish and hunt.

Sieh-li, having succeeded in his Eastern Expedition, has become the generalissimo and has started on his way back to share his glory with his wife. At Fên Hê Wan he meets his son. He is so interested in the skill of the unknown youth that he cannot help stopping to look at him. Suddenly he sees a tiger at some distance behind the boy and intending to save the latter aims his arrow at the beast. By some ill fate, the boy is shot.

Very distressed, he rides on until he comes before his old cave, where he sees a woman sitting outside as if she were waiting for somebody. Neither recognizes the other (Illus. 34, 49), but when Sieh-li finds that she is his wife, he decides to test her loyalty by posing as his friend who has bought her to be his wife. She stands the test well and they are happily re-united, until Sieh-li finds a man's slipper under her bed. He is so angry that he immediately draws his sword to kill her (Illus. 75). She is not vexed nor frightened at all, but amused at her husband's unfounded suspicion (Illus. 52). She plays with him saying that the owner of the slipper is much more handsome and thoughtful than he. She would have starved had he not helped her. Finally she makes known the identity of the boy and goes on praising her son as being the only youth in the vicinity who has such wonderful military skill. The father is horrified and tells her of the tragic accident at Fên Hê Wan. The play ends with a grief-stricken search for the boy's body.

Gramophone Records available:

Tan ....by	Mei Lan-fang	(梅 蘭 芳)	....	*Pathé*
„ .... „	Ch'êng Yen-ts'iu	(程 硯 秋)	....	*Great Wall*
„ .... „	„	„	....	*Odeon*
Shên .... „	Yen Chü-pêng	(言 菊 朋)	....	„
„ .... „	Wang Yu-ch'un	(王 又 宸)	....	*Victor*
„ .... „	Loo Hsiao-pao	(羅 小 寶)	....	*Great China*
Tan and Shên ...... „	⎰Ch'êng Yen-ts'iu			
	⎱Wang Shau-lou	(王 少 樓)	....	*Beka*

LOVE WINS WHERE DISCIPLINE FAILS

or YÜAN MÊN TSAI TZŬ

（轅 門 斬 子）

While Yang Yen-chao was trying to conquer Mu, a bandit chief in Shantung province, because he was desperately in need of the "Chiang-lung" wood, grown on Mu's lands, he was embarrassingly defeated by Mu's daughter, Kuei-ing. He had to camp where he was and wait for an opportunity to steal the wood.

One night while Yang Tsung-pao, his only son, was on sentry duty, two elderly generals induced him to steal into Mu Kuei-ing's camp and challenge her, for they thought that the young general might be able to win. His efforts failed and he was caught and held in captivity. Kuei-ing, falling in love with him, offered him the choice of marrying her or of being put to death. He chose death, but later when he thought of being his father's only son and of Kuei-ing's promise to furnish him with the desired precious wood, he agreed to the marriage. A hasty wedding took place.

The next day the young general returned to his father, and found him in great wrath. He had sentenced his son to death for having married the bandit's daughter. In spite of the petitions of all the subordinate generals, the Emperor's brother and even his own mother, Yang Yen-chao insisted on the execution.

Finally the bride, Kuei-ing (Illus. 21), came herself. She threatened to fight against Yang Yen-chao in person, if he carried out the execution, and at the same time she offered to furnish the "Chiang-lung"[1] wood, if her husband were released. Partly in fear of the tigress and partly because of the urgent need for the valuable wood, the old general reluctantly yielded to the bargain. The play ends with the bride's remark to her father-in-law, "Even though you do not love him, I do!"

Gramophone Records available:

Lao-shên	.............by	Liu Hung-shên	(劉 鴻 聲)	.............*Pathé*
„	.... „	Loo Lan-ch'un	(羅 蘭 春)	.............*Victor*
„	.... „	Kao Chun-ku'ei	(高 慶 奎)	.............*Odeon*
„	.... „	Yen Chü-pêng	(言 菊 朋)	.... „
„	.... „	Kwok Ts'ong-heng	(郭 仲 衡)	.... „
„	.... „	Ma Lien-liang	(馬 連 良)	.............*Beka*
„	.... „	Kuan Ta-yüan	(貫 大 元)	.............*Great China*
Lao-tan	.... „	Lee Too-ku'ei	(李 多 奎)	.............*Beka*

---

[1] The literal meaning of "Chiang-lung" (降 龍) is "to conquer the dragon." This wood was used in fighting against the strategic troop arrangement of the enemy, called "tien-mên-tsen" (天 門 陣), a fatal trap for those who did not know how to get out.

LOYALTY FINDS A WAY
or YÜ CHOU FÊNG
（宇 宙 鋒）

About 200 B.C. during the reign of Er-Shih, there was a vicious premier, Chao Kao, who had a very good and charming daughter. Though she never agreed with her father's way of living, she obediently married K'uang Fu, the man of her father's choice and the son of a faithful, upright minister, K'uang Hung, the bitter enemy of the premier. The marriage was forced upon the K'uang family by the premier, through a mandate by the Emperor, in order that the daughter might be used as a spy. She performed her duties as a wife and a daughter-in-law so faithfully that her father was greatly disappointed.

Chao Kao, therefore, sent a man to steal K'uang Hung's "Yü Chou Fêng" (literally, the sword of the universe), a priceless gift from the Emperor. Then he directed him to pretend to assassinate the Emperor with the sword but to leave it and make his escape so as to throw suspicion upon K'uang Hung as the real assassin. The plan was a success and old K'uang Hung was imprisoned and the son had to flee for his life. In order to delay pursuit, a faithful servant whose appearance was similar to K'uang Fu volunteered to kill himself, thus making the Emperor believe that the young man was dead. The wretched daughter, now left homeless, had to return to her father's house as a widow. One night the Emperor came to visit the premier in disguise and saw the lovely lady. At once he ordered the father to send her to the palace next morning to be his favourite. Chao Kao was

Illus. 76. An Aside. *Left to right:* The Maid (by Chu Kuei-fang) ; The Lady
(by Mei Lan-fang) ; The Emperor (by Wang Shau-t'ing) ;
The Father (by Liu Lien-yung)

PLAY: *Loyalty Finds a Way*

only too willing to be thus elevated to the position of being the Emperor's father-in-law. (Note: The father of the Emperor's concubine might be called father-law of the sovereign.)

The daughter pleaded in vain against the decision, and quarrelled with her father. She reminded him that according to custom she should obey her parents as to her first marriage, but that the right of choosing a second husband belonged to none other than herself and that since she had done her duty in marrying the man of his choice, she had a perfect right to refuse to obey him the second time. Still Chao Kao insisted that she should obey the Emperor, if not him, and that disobedience would mean death. The loyal wife chose death! Her maid, however, who was dumb, showed her that a pretense of insanity might save her from being taken by the lustful ruler. She followed the maid's suggestion: tore her dress, threw away her shoes, let her hair down, bruised herself, pulled her father's beard (see Illus. 44), addressed and caressed him as if he were her husband, and finally declared that she had been summoned by the gods to ascend to Heaven (see Illus. 48).

Very embarrassed and distressed, Chao Kao reported to the Emperor that his daughter had suddenly become insane. It was not so easy to make the lascivious tyrant give her up; she must prove that she was really insane. She was therefore summoned to the palace to be examined by the Emperor (Illus. 76). In wild strains of insanity, she appeared before the Emperor, calling him brother emperor at one time and base tyrant at another, and addressing Chao Kao, her father, as her darling son (Illus. 40). The dissimulation was so well portrayed that finally the Emperor was convinced and the loyal beauty was sent home.

Gramophone Records available:

Tan ....by	Mei Lan-fang	(梅 蘭 芳)..............*Great China*
,, ... ,,	,,	,, ...*Victor*
,, ... ,,	,,	,, ...*Odeon*
,, ... ,,	,,	,, ...*Beka*
Tan and Shên .... ,,	{ Chiang Miao-hsiang	(姜 妙 香)..............*Victor*

Illus. 77.   A Posture in the Tray and Winepot Dance (by Mei Lan-fang)

PLAY: *Ma-ku Offering Birthday Greetings*

MA-KU OFFERING BIRTHDAY GREETINGS

or MA-KU HSIEN SHOU

（麻 姑 獻 壽）

NOTE:—*Ma-ku has been popularly taken to represent the goddess who offers long life to every woman on her birthday. Usually, her picture is hung in the main celebration hall. At birthday parties, this play is always an appropriate item on the programme.*

The play opens with all the fairies busily preparing for the celebration of the third of March, the birthday of the leading goddess, Mother Wang. One of them named Ma-ku starts out to pick the precious, rare flowers and herbs to be distilled into the Everlasting Wine which she plans to offer as her birthday present.

The actor dances in both the flower-gathering and the birthday celebration scenes. In the latter, the sleeve dance (Illus. 37) and the tray and winepot dance (Illus. 77) give the most spectacular and aesthetic effects.

Gramophone Record available:

Tan ....,.....by Mei Lan-fang （梅 蘭 芳）....................*Victor*

Illus. 78.   Mei Lan-fang in the Rôle of Mu-lan

PLAY: *Mu-lan, the Disguised Warrior Maiden*

MU-LAN, THE DISGUISED WARRIOR MAIDEN

or MU-LAN TS'UNG CHÜN

（木 蘭 從 軍）

NOTE:—*The source of this play is an old, well-known poem entitled "Mu-lan." The play consists of two parts, and is usually given on two successive nights.*

PART I.

China was invaded by a northern tribe, named T"u Chüeh, and the Emperor ordered conscription to be enforced all over the country. Hua Wu, a veteran, had two elder daughters and a little son. He was old and just convalescing from a long and serious illness. The whole family—especially the second daughter, Mu-lan—worried over his joining the army. For months she had been unable to weave as her time was spent in caring for her father. The play opens with Mu-lan resuming her weaving after her father's convalescence.

She was so deep in thought considering the problem of how to relieve her father that she sighed and absent-mindedly left her weaving (see p. 144, Item XVII). Mu-wei, her elder sister, surprised at her queer behaviour, teased her for being love-lorn. Mu-lan then disclosed the cause of her worry, saying, "Sister, not every girl sighs for want of love. Now, you too, sigh when you think of father's predicament. Are you eager to find a lover?"

One morning when a messenger came to summon Hua Wu (Illus. 5), Mu-lan, having dressed herself in her father's armour and helmet and carrying his spear (Illus. 59), was ready to set out in his place. In spite of her family's objection, Mu-lan won the argument by telling them of her past preparations and by showing them her ability to use the spear.

PART II.

For twelve years her comrades failed to discover that she was a woman. Once in a hot battle, she saved the life of the Commander-in-chief and won promotion. Later she accomplished so many deeds of valour that she was finally made a major-general.

One night, while on watch, she noticed some excited birds flying overhead. She realized at once that the enemy must be marching secretly toward her camp. She immediately reported to the Commander-in-chief and proposed to send a group of men to steal forth to a strategic point and lie in ambush so that when the hostile army passed, their return could be blocked. Her plan was followed and when the T'u Chüeh tribesmen came, they had to face Mu-lan's men on all four sides. There was no way for them to retreat or to advance, and they were entirely routed.

As a conquering hero, Mu-lan rejected all the Emperor's rewards except a steed to carry her home immediately. Approaching her native village, she spied an old man sitting on a rock near the entrance, as if he were waiting for someone. She rode up closer and lo, he was her dear father! For years he had come to this place to wait for the return of his filial child. She was welcomed immediately. Her people could hardly recognize the disguised soldier as the former Mu-lan. The little brother had become a grown man. Big feasts were spread and everybody was proud of her. She returned to her own bedchamber and once more put on her maiden attire.

Honours and presents from the Emperor were bestowed upon this wonderful general whom the messengers, to their surprise, found to be just a young maiden. She distributed the presents among her former soldier comrades and expressed her desire to lead a simple, rural life with her parents.

Gramophone Records available:

Hsiao-shên	.... by Mei Lan-fang	(梅 蘭 芳)	*Pathé*
,,	.... ,, Hsu Pih-yuin	(徐 碧 雲)	*Victor*
,,	.... ,, Chiang Miao-hsiang	(姜 妙 香)	,,
,,	.... ,, ,,	,, ...	*Pathé*

A NUN¹ SEEKS LOVE

or SZŬ FAN

（思 凡）

NOTE:—*This is a romantic, one-act play of the K'un-ch'u type, and is given by the "tan" alone. The actor dances and sings to the accompaniment of the flute.*

A beautiful young maiden, on account of poor health, had been sent in childhood to a convent by her superstitious parents, who had believed that she could enjoy long life only by being offered to the gods (Illus. 79). As usual, romantic ideas crept into the mind of this girl. She could not endure solitude but greatly desired to have a mate. She saw that even the gods were laughing at her for thus wasting her precious youth.

"Who will be willing to marry an old woman?" she questioned herself. "What will become of me when I am old and stooping?" So, finally, she threw away the sacred book and the cymbals with which she sang; tore apart her nun's robe and fled down the mountain to find some young lover, with whom to settle down. She longed to own a cosy little home and, maybe, some day have fine children.

Gramophone Record available:

Tan................by Miss Chang （張 五 小 姐）..................*Pathé*

---

¹ The nun always holds a horse-hair duster (Illus. 14), which is a highly-esteemed object to represent persons of refinement. In Chinese drama only those who play the servant class, such as the lower eunuchs or maid-servants, use it in dusting. The others, that is, those who play gods, goddesses, spirits, nuns, monks, etc. hold it to represent their exalted position.

Illus. 79.   The Nun at Worship (by Mei Lan-fang)

PLAY: *A Nun Seeks Love*

THE PASS OF CHAO NO. I
or "CIVIL" CHAO KWAN
（文 昭 關）

The King of Ch'u was so lascivious that he drove out his son and proceeded to take his wife as one of his concubines. His upright minister, Wu Sheh, strongly advised that at least the king should let the daughter-in-law alone. The king's flatterer, Fei, suggested to the king that he throw the "unscrupulous minister" into prison for insulting his sovereign, but fearing Wu's two tiger sons serving as generals on the frontier might seek revenge, forged a king's mandate (see p. 23, Item 3) ordering Wu to write a letter to summon the young men to the capital. A friend discovered the intrigue and secretly informed the brothers.

Wu Shang the elder, told Wu Yuin (more popularly known as Wu Tzŭ-sü) that since it was their father's letter, they must obey, but the younger replied, "I doubt if it is father's genuine intention to summon us into this trap, so I will stay behind and plan revenge if anything should happen to you or father."

When news came that his father and brother were actually murdered and that Fei had ordered his picture to be hung at every city gate of the kingdom, offering liberal rewards to any who would arrest him, Wu Yuin decided to flee to the Kingdom of Wu, whose king was the bitter enemy of the King of Ch'u.

First of all he must get through the Pass of Chao. He hid himself in his friend's home and next morning it was discovered that he looked like a different man! Excitement and worry had in one night made his hair and beard entirely white! A bright idea came to the friend. He immediately sent for a man, named Wong-fu Nê, who looked somewhat like Wu Yuin.

The next morning Wong-fu was found trying to slip through the Pass of Chao and was mistaken by the gatekeepers for Wu. He argued in such a way that the gatekeepers became more and more positive that he was the fugitive. In the midst of this turmoil the white-haired Wu slipped through the Pass just as the friend was starting on his way to prove that the arrested man was not Wu Yuin but Wong-fu, one of his close friends.

Gramophone Records available:

Lao-shèn . . . . by Wang Feng-chun (王 鳳 卿) . . . . *Beka*

  ,, ... ,,   ,,   ,, ... *Great China*

  ,, ... ,, Yen Chü-pêng (言 菊 朋) . . . . *Victor*

  . . . . ,, Mêng Poo-tsar (孟 曹 齋) . . . . ,,

THE PASS OF CHAO NO. II

or "MILITARY" CHAO KWAN

（武 昭 關）

The King of Ch'u was lascivious to such a degree that he drove away his own son and was about to make his beautiful daughter-in-law one of his concubines, when General Wu Yuin forced his way into the palace and rescued the lady and her son, the baby prince. They fled from the capital together. Seeing the king's men in hot pursuit, they had to take refuge temporarily in a big monastery. Realizing that General Wu was already worn out and crestfallen and that apparently it would be impossible for him to rescue both the child and herself, the mother put the prince in the general's care and jumped into a nearby well (see p. 147, Item XXII), thus hoping to lessen the burden of General Wu. Though the noble general unfortunately failed to rescue the lady, he succeeded in getting through the Pass of Chao, to a country where he and the baby prince might enjoy peace and liberty.

Gramophone Records available:

Tan ....by Mei Lan-fang	（梅 蘭 芳）................*Victor*
,, ... ,,	................*Great China*
,, ... ,, Ch'êng Yü-tsin	（程 玉 菁）................*Beka*
Lao-shên .... ,, Lin Shŭ-shên	（林 樹 森）................*Victor*

235

Illus. 80.   A Posture in the Flute and Plume Dance (by Chu Kuei-fang
and Mei Lan-fang)   ·

PLAY: *The Patriotic Beauty, Hsi Shih*

THE PATRIOTIC BEAUTY
or HSI SHIH

（西 施）

NOTE:—*"Hsi" means "west." It is said that there were two villages, all of whose residents were surnamed Shih. Hsi Shih, one of the four most famous beauties of ancient China, lived in the western Shih village, hence her name.*

After the decisive battle between the ever war-waging kingdoms of Wu and Yueh, Kou-tsien, the king of the latter kingdom was taken prisoner by Fu-ch'a, the king of the former. Liberal bribes and the captive's wit succeeded in making the foolish conqueror grant the release of the prisoner. Upon returning to his own kingdom Kou-tsien slept on a straw bed and tasted bitter gall every morning so as to remind himself of the shame that he had experienced during his captivity.

Fan Lee, his Prime Minister, set out to find the most beautiful maiden in the kingdom and finally he found Hsi Shih, a matchless beauty, who because of poverty was forced to earn a humble living by bleaching yarn. She was, however, rich in intelligence and patriotism and consented to co-operate with Fan Lee and sacrifice herself for her king and country.

She was presented to Fu-ch'a with a number of ladies-in-waiting and before long she succeeded in fascinating the conqueror of her country. The great king's attention, paid formerly to affairs of state, was now transferred to the graceful dances (Illus. 80) of this charming favourite. Splendid palaces were put up just to please her. The best known structure erected for her was the "Echoing Corridor" (響 屧 廊), which was so built that when Hsi Shih walked or danced along it, the king could enjoy the pleasing echoes of her mincing steps. (Today any tourist who visits Lin-yen Hill, about five miles west of the city of

Illus. 81.   The Fan Dance (by Mei Lan-fang)
PLAY: *The Patriotic Beauty, Hsi Shih*

Soochow, Kiangsu Province, can find the old site of the platform where the king and Hsi Shih used to sit on summer nights, and also the pool whose water served as a mirror for the lady when she arranged her pretty, dark hair.)

Gradually, through neglect, the kingdom of Wu grew weaker and weaker, whereas the kingdom of Yueh never allowed the people rest, but kept them always busy strengthening their military forces, developing resources to maintain a large standing army and working in every way to make the country more progressive.

Discovering that the kingdom of Wu was declining, the vassal king of T'si refused to send tribute.   Upon Hsi Shih's persuasion, the pleasure-loving king led an expensive punitive expedition against T'si, and while both men and money were being spent on that unworthy cause, Kou-tsien, now well-equipped, led his armies forward and with the help of the patriotic beauty, entered the capital easily.   The homeless Fu-ch'a felt so humiliated and desperate that he committed suicide, and Hsi Shih was welcomed home with pomp and splendour.

The play ends as the Prime Minister, Fan Lee, and the long admired Hsi Shih, his bride, retire from public life.   In this last scene, the two actors, each holding an oar, dance around, posturing in harmony with the movements of the imaginary little boat (see pp. 144-145, Items XVIII-XIX).

Gramophone Records available:

Tan	by Mei Lan-fang	(梅 蘭 芳)...............	Pathé
,, ...	,, ,,	,, ...	Victor
,, ...	,, ,,	,, ...	Odeon
Hsiao-shên	,, Chiang Miao-hsiang	(姜 妙 香)...............	,,
,, ...	,, ,,	,, ...	Beka

Illus. 82. The Spear Dance (by Mei Lan-fang)

PLAY: *The Rainbow Pass*

DATE:

A.D. 560-580

THE RAINBOW PASS
or HUNG NI KWAN
（虹 霓 關）

NOTE:—*In Part I, the leading actor plays the widow, the character being a "tao-ma-tan," but in Part II he takes the rôle of "hua-tan."*

Toward the close of the sixth century China was overrun by a number of war-lords, among whom was the valiant general, Lee Mi. In the midst of his conquests, he was fiercely confronted by another courageous warrior, Sin Wên-li. Lee sent Wang Pê-tang, an expert archer, to take Rainbow Pass, the impregnable stronghold of Sin. The latter was superior to Wang as a fighter but was not so clever a strategist; eventually he was tricked and killed by the fatal arrow of the bowman.

Sin's brave and charming widow, Tung-fang, swore vengeance upon her husband's murderer. Therefore, she ordered her man to go to the battlefield with her in mourning (Illus. 61, 82). She declared that she would place Wang's head before Sin's coffin as an offering.

Her avenging spirit, however, did not last long. The moment she saw the handsome enemy, she was deeply infatuated (Illus. 83). Feigning defeat she led the young archer into the trap she had set, and made him her prisoner. (Part I ends here.)

Part II opens with the victorious return of the heroine. To all of Sin's followers it seemed that the fate of the bowman was definitely sealed. So thought the widow's smart maid (Illus. 84). Not until the loyal maid had urged her mistress for a long time to fulfil her oath, did Tung-fang reveal her intention of marrying the prisoner.

241

Illus. 83. The Spear Dance. "Tan" (by Mei Lan-fang); "Shên"
(by Chu Kuei-fang)
PLAY: *The Rainbow Pass*

At first, the ingenious maid tried to persuade her mistress to abide by her oath, but upon realizing that Tung-fang's mad passion was genuine, she consented to be her match-maker.   The young man chose death to marriage, unless Tung-fang would submit to his conditions:

(1)   She must place a banner of surrender on the city wall;

(2)   She must welcome all of his colleagues into her land;

(3)   The actual wedding must not take place until three days after the wedding celebration.

The widow was only too willing to consent, and she herself freed Wang from chains.   The play ends with a hasty wedding.

Gramophone Records available:

Tan	.... by Mei Lan-fang	（梅 蘭 芳）...............	*Pathé*
,,	.... ,, Chên Tê-lin	（陳 德 霖）...............	*Odeon*
,,	.... ,, Sün Hui-shên	（荀 慧 生）.............. ...	,,
,,	.... ,, Shang Hsiao-yuin	（尙 小 雲）...............	*Great Wall*
,,	.... ,, Chang Ngê-yuin	（章 遏 雲）.............,....	*Victor*
,,	.... ,, Hsu Pih-yuin	（徐 碧 雲）...............	*Beka*

Illus. 84. A Scene in "The Rainbow Pass" (*Left to right*) 1—The Maid
(by Ch'èng Yen-ts'iu); 2—The Widow (by Shang Hsiao-yuin);
3—The Hero (by Mei Lan-fang, playing that rôle in jest)

THE RED-MANED STEED
or HUNG TSONG LIEH MA
（紅 鬃 烈 馬）

NOTE:—*This story is the source of the recent very popular play, "Lady Precious Stream." It consists of eleven parts, each part often being given as a separate performance. If the entire story is presented on one night, it will take about seven-and-a-half hours (from 6 p.m.—1:30 a.m.). The best actors do not appear until late on the programme, and this results in the reserved seats in the theatre being seldom occupied during the first seven parts.*

PART I.   HOW WANG PAO-CH'UAN CHOSE HER HUSBAND
or TS'AI LOU P'EI （彩 樓 配）

Wang Yuin, the Prime Minister, had three daughters, among whom Pao-ch'uan, the youngest, was the loveliest and best educated. Her parents were so proud of her that they arranged to let her choose her own husband. They had a tower (see p. 27, Item 20) erected and decorated with flowers.   On the appointed day the lady was to stand inside and throw down the beautiful five-coloured embroidered ball, a special gift from the Emperor for the occasion, to the youth of her choice.   The day before the betrothal she was walking in her garden, where she found a beggar fast asleep.   His clear-cut features struck her as giving promise that he would become a great man some day. After further investigation, she discovered that he, Sieh P'ing-kuei, was a genius in military tactics and was now poor only because he had no opportunity to work.   She told him of the incident that would take place the next day and asked him to come to try his fortune, and gave him some gold with which to buy clothes.

The next morning there was much excitement before the tower; nobles, officials and scholars gathered there hoping to receive the ball. The choice fell on the beggar, and Sieh was claimed as the fiance of the lovely maiden.

Gramophone Records available:

Tan .... by Mei Lan-fang （梅 蘭 芳）.................. *Great Wall*
  „   .... „ Chên Tê-lin   （陳 德 霖）.................. *Odeon*

PART II. THE WAGER or SAN CHI CHANG (三擊掌)

The Prime Minister refused to consent to the marriage, because Sieh belonged to the lowest caste. The daughter, however, insisted that fate might not be averted by man's will, not even her father's. For the first time father and daughter quarrelled. In spite of the mother's advice, the girl accepted her father's challenge to leave home at once, penniless, and never to return until fate had made her a rich lady of high rank. They clapped each other's hands three times to confirm the agreement. Then she took off the gorgeous robe and jewelry, sorrowfully bade goodbye to her mother and followed Sieh to his home which was a cave on the side of a hill.

Gramophone Record available:

Tan ....by Ch'êng Yen-ts'iu (程硯秋)...............*Great China*

PART III. SIEH, THE HERO, JOINS THE ARMY
or T'OU CHUN PIEH YAO (投軍別窰)

The grateful husband now felt it more urgent than ever to find a position so that he could support his wife, but failed again and again. One day he succeeded in conquering some dreadful monster, which was, in fact, a fierce wild horse, which was so unapproachable and whose mane was so long and red that it looked like some strange beast with a red fur coat. On account of its great strength many men whom it had kicked died instantly. Placards were posted and liberal rewards were offered to successful volunteers. Sieh tamed the horse and named it "The Red-maned Steed." This deed of valour started his great career by giving him the opportunity to enter the army. Before leaving he sadly asked his bride to give up the wager and return home, because his future was very uncertain. In tears the lady replied, "I would rather starve than return to my father. I shall wait for your return and for the day when I can show my father who you are." Deeply touched, Sieh assured her of his determination to make her dream come true and reluctantly left for the enlisting headquarters where he discovered that he had been put under the command of Soo and Wei, the husbands of his wife's elder sisters, who had been instructed by the Prime Minister to murder Sieh. Fortunately Soo refused to obey the order, but on the contrary tried his best to help the young man, while Wei, aiming to win Pao-ch'uan for his second wife, exerted himself to carry out the father's wish.

Gramophone Record available:

Shên and Tan ....by ⎰Lin Shŭ-shên   (林 樹 森)
                        ⎱Wang Yuin-fang (王 芸 芳)...............*Victor*

PART IV. PAO-CH'UAN REFUSES TO STOOP
or T'AN HAN YAO (探 寒 窰)

News came back that Sieh was dead and word was sent to the lady by her father asking her to give up the wager, return home, marry a man of her own rank, and lead an easy, happy life. Pao-ch'uan gave no answer and remained in poverty. Indeed, she would have starved had her mother not secretly continued to support her.

When the kind mother first went to visit her daughter, she insisted on her return, for the cave seemed uninhabitable, and when Pao-ch'uan refused to leave, the mother threatened that she too would live in the cave to keep her company. The frightened daughter cleverly feigned to promise to follow her home. As soon as the mother and her servants stepped out, she bolted the door and knelt inside,[1] begging the mother to pardon her disobedience. She declared that she was determined to abide by the agreement, so the old lady, disappointed but admiring her child's self sacrifice, had to return home alone.

Gramophone Records available:

Tan ....by Chiang Ch'un-cha (蔣 君 稼)...............*Beka*
Lao-tan .... „ Lee Too-ku'ei   (李 多 奎)..............*Great China*
  „   .... „ Wo-yuin-chü-shih (臥 雲 居 士)............*Victor*

PART V. SIEH'S SECOND MARRIAGE
or SI LIANG CH'AO TS'IN (西 凉 招 親)

Though Wei had again and again sent Sieh to fight at very dangerous points, every time the latter, with the help of the wonderful steed,

---

[1] The actor kneels behind a chair to represent that "she" is inside the imaginary door. In this play the pantomime of bolting and unbolting the door is just the same as that in "The Suspicious Slipper."

returned victor. Finally, Wei invited him to a big feast in celebration of his chivalrous achievements and induced him to drink so much that he became intoxicated. Then the rascal bound him on his steed and with the war drums sounding drove him forward towards the enemy. He was taken captive and later would have been executed had he not been rescued by the Princess Ta Ts'â, the only daughter of the King of Si Liang, whose heart he had unconsciously won by his valiant deeds on the battlefield. She treated him so well that he finally surrendered to her successive offers of marriage. Thus he became the son and heir to the throne of Si Liang.

PART VI. THE BROKEN-HEARTED MESSAGE
or HUNG YEN CH'UAN SHU (鴻 雁 傳 書)

Spring after spring the lady, Pao-ch'uan, watched for the return of the early birds. She did not believe the news that Wei had brought back, for she knew that the latter wanted her hand, yet after the lapse of eighteen springs, she did begin to doubt that her husband would ever return. She was so broken-hearted and lonely that she began to talk with the birds, asking if any of them would carry a letter to Sieh in Si Liang. Strangely enough one bird nodded its head as if consenting to render her the service. (This is portrayed by an actor standing on a chair and holding a silk bird which nods to the lady.) Then she tore off a strip from her dress, bit her finger and writing the letter in blood, begged Sieh to come back to her ere she die of a broken heart. She tied the message to the bird's leg (the lady hands the strip to the actor who holds the bird) and it flew away.

PART VII. SIEH RETURNS HOME or KAN SAN KWAN (趕 三 關)

In his new home Sieh had not dared to reveal his true life history to the old king or his daughter. When he succeeded to the throne, he knew that as a foreign king he was forbidden to enter the territory of his own country.

One morning just after the regular state session, he saw a bird nodding as if addressing him and looking at it more closely he noticed the strip of cloth. Reading the message on it he was so ashamed that he immediately sent for the Princess—now the Queen. He made her drunk and secretly left for his homeland on his faithful "Red-maned Steed." He passed through the three strategic posts in disguise with his own mandate arrow as his "passport" (see p. 23, Item 2). When he reached the border, he was overtaken by the Princess to whom he was now compelled to tell the truth. His story won her sympathy and she not only let him go on but gave him a trained dove to send back to her in case of danger.

Gramophone Records available:

Tan ....by Chên Tê-lin (陳 德 霖)................*Pathé*
„ and Shên .... „ ⎰Tan Foo-ing (譚 富 英)
⎱Wang Yuin-fang (王 芸 芳)................ „

PART VIII. THE MEETING AT WU CHIA PU
or WU CHIA PU (武 家 坡)

NOTE:—*This part is one of the most popular plays on the Chinese stage. The dialogue and songs are very much the same as those in "The Suspicious Slipper."*

A neighbour brought word to Pao-ch'uan that a messenger from her husband was waiting for her at Wu Chia Pu. She hurried there only to find a soldier (Illus. 85), who claimed to be her second husband, the man to whom Sieh had sold her. She refused to admit the legality of such a contract and after quarrelling with him she ran back home. The disguised soldier was none other than Sieh himself. Seeing that his wife stood well the test of fidelity, he quickly identified himself and knelt before her, begging forgiveness. Since this was the most humiliating way of begging pardon, the lady willingly let the eighteen years of suffering be offset by this mere bending of the husband's precious knees! (An old Chinese proverb says: "There is gold under man's knees; he cannot bend them before a woman").

Gramophone Records available:

Tan and Shên ....by ⎰Ch'êng Yen-ts'iu (程 硯 秋)
⎱Tan Foo-ing (譚 富 英)..............*Victor*
„ „ „ .... „ ⎰Shang Hsiao-yuin (尚 小 雲)..............*Great Wall*
⎱Wang Shau-lou (王 少 樓)..............*Odeon*

Illus. 85.   The Aside Sleeve (by the Author and her schoolmate)
PLAY: *The Meeting at Wu Chia Pu*

PART IX. CLEARING OF ACCOUNTS or SÜAN LIANG (算 糧)

The lady was now ready to return to her father, but she waited till his birthday came. Alone and in ragged clothes, she went to give her father birthday greetings. The Prime Minister and Wei thought she had changed her mind and was returning home to live, but the first thing she did after the ceremony was to demand from Wei the legal monthly allowance due her husband during the past eighteen years. They began to quarrel and Sieh was summoned to testify to Wei's perfidy. Finally they all decided to put the case before the Emperor.

PART X. NEMESIS BEGINS HER WORK
or YIN K'UNG SHAN (銀 空 山)

Just as the Prime Minister, Wei and Sieh reached the palace, the bell began to toll the death of the old Emperor, so Sieh had to postpone the settlement until a later date. The Prime Minister quickly attempted to usurp the throne with Wei as his chief colleague in the conspiracy. Sieh immediately sent back the dove to the Princess who marched her troops to the capital before the rebellious army could be prepared to resist her. A sweeping victory ended the rebel's career, made Sieh the Emperor and the conspirators his prisoners.

PART XI. THE FINAL SCORE or HUI LUNG KÊ (迴 龍 閣)

The new Emperor himself sat in judgment on the rebels. He ordered that the treacherous Prime Minister be the first to be executed for treason. Just then Pao-ch'uan—now the Empress—challenged the Emperor saying that if her father's life was not spared she would die with him. Though the Emperor felt the request was too great, yet he consented to the acquittal. The old man was allowed to come back to the audience hall to express his gratitude to the Emperor and Empress.

Here the "tan" (the Empress) sings one of the most exquisite songs in the whole play. She relates how her belief in fate was justified and that though her husband was exceedingly poor at the time of her betrothal, yet the beggar had won his title and she the wager.

Then she urged the Emperor to bring Wei to trial. She severely reprimanded him before his decapitation and ordered that his head be hoisted on a spike. After the trial, the Princess Ta Ts'â was introduced to the Empress by the embarrassed husband. The ladies soon became good friends and sisters. They agreed to summon the Empress' mother to come to the palace to live and the old man was left alone in the Pension House. A happy ending closes this much loved drama.

Gramophone Records available:

Tan ....by	Ch'êng Yen-ts'iu	（程 硯 秋）...............*Pathé*
„ .... „	„	„ ....*Victor*
„ .... „	Hsüeh Yen-ch'in	（雪 艷 琴）...............*Odeon*
Lao-tan .... „	Wo-yuin-chü-shih	（臥 雲 居 士）.............*Beka*
„ shên .... „	Yen Chü-p'êng	（言 菊 朋）...............*Odeon*
Shên and Tan .... „ { Sin Yen-ts'iu	„	（新 艷 秋）...............*Pathé*

THE REWARD OF KINDNESS

or CHU SHA CHIH

(行善得子即硃砂痣)

Han, a rich old widower, whose wife and only son were lost during the invasion by the northern barbarians twelve years before, was now ready to buy himself a concubine so that he might not be without an heir.

On removing the "bridal headcover,"[1] Han found that the bride looked broken-hearted and sad. When questioned, the poor woman told him that she had sold herself in order to pay the medical expenses of her husband who was seriously ill. The kind man immediately set her free, sent her back to her husband and gave the couple one hundred taels of silver (1 tael=Sh. $1.40).

The gift and the return of his wife cured the patient and on the very next day the overjoyed couple came to thank Han. They soon learned that the rich man's one desire was to have a child. Therefore, they not only advised Han to adopt a son, but after having conducted some business abroad and made some profit, brought back a smart, handsome boy and presented him to their benefactor.

Not long after the adoption, a red mark on the boy's left foot was discovered exactly like that on the left foot of his long-lost son. Han concluded that his generosity had brought back his own offspring.

Gramophone Records available:

Lao-shên ....by Wang Feng-chun (王 鳳 卿)................*Beka*
    ,, ...,, Liu Shu-tu   (劉 叔 度).................*Victor*

---

[1] According to the old Chinese custom, every bride wears an almost square piece of red silk, so as to hide her face. In the case of rich brides, it is beautifully embroidered.

Because Chiang Shao was often away from home on business, Chiang Ts'iu-lien, his daughter by a former marriage, was left at the mercy of her step-mother. One day the latter ordered Ts'iu-lien to go to the woods to gather fuel, but as it was not considered proper for maidens of well-to-do families to do manual labour, Ts'iu-lien preferred to stay at home and study. She was severely whipped for disobedience, so her old nurse persuaded her to get the fuel.

On the way they met a handsome young scholar by the name of Lee Ch'un-fa, who, seeing that they did not belong to the labouring class, inquired what they were doing. The nurse, suspecting he was trying to flirt with her mistress, reprimanded him. To prove his innocence the scholar put some silver on the ground, asked them to buy fuel with it, and then went away without telling them his name.

Ts'iu-lien was so grateful that she sent the the nurse to call him back. During the conversation the maiden blushingly asked him whether he had been married or not. He felt greatly embarrassed and left immediately.

When the two women reached home they gave the step-mother the silver and told her frankly about the young man. The wicked step-mother accused Ts'iu-lien of unchastity and threatened to kill her. In terror, the maiden fled with her nurse. At midnight they met a highwayman who not only murdered the nurse and robbed them of all they had, but started to violate the maiden. The latter declared that she belonged to a high-bred family and that she must have a witness before she became his wife. She looked around and chose a red flower, growing on the cliff nearby, to be their witness. As soon as the robber stooped down, Ts'iu-lien pushed him down into the gorge.

Usually the play ends with Ts'iu-lien's narrow escape, but the story goes on with the step-mother's prosecution of the scholar for the seduction of Ts'iu-lien, the latter's entrance into a convent and finally the marriage of the hero and heroine.

Only Mei Lan-fang (梅 蘭 芳) has given this play in full. In recent years he, too, has concluded the play at the climax, *i.e.* the escape.

Gramophone Records available:

Tan ....by Mei Lan-fang　　(梅 蘭 芳) ....*Victor*
„ ....„ Shang Hsiao-yuin　(尙 小 雲) ....*Pathé*

Illus. 86.   A Scene in "The Royal Monument Pavilion"

(by the Author and her friend)

THE ROYAL MONUMENT PAVILION

or YU PEI T'ING

(御 碑 亭)

Mêng Yü-hua after seeing her husband, Wang You-tao, off to the capital to take the imperial examinations, was asked to go home to attend her family's ancestral worship. Because her young sister-in-law would be left alone, she refused to go, but, after continued persuasion by the sister (Illus. 86) and her father's servant, she went home on the understanding that she would be back before dark.

After the worship, though her parents insisted on her staying with them, she left the room, pretending that she had to retire because of illness. Secretly she slipped out through the backgarden. Before she was half-way home, a terrible thunderstorm overtook her and she was compelled to take shelter at the Royal Monument Pavilion.

Not long afterwards, a young scholar, named Liu, happened to come to that same pavilion for shelter. Seeing the beautiful lady he started to leave so as not to annoy her at such a late hour (the old idea being that the sexes should not associate). Then, thinking that after his departure some rascal might come to molest her, he stayed under the eaves of the pavilion so that he could be her protector. This noble act was duly recorded by the four sentinel gods in heaven (portrayed by actors standing on chairs with pen and paper in hand), who later influenced the Chief Examiner to choose Liu and put his essay, which had been rejected three times previously, among the winning compositions.

Not until dawn did Yü-hua reach her husband's home. She frankly told her sister-in-law of the pavilion incident. The innocent maiden teased her, saying that it was the will of heaven that she had the chance to meet the handsome young scholar, but Yü-hua took it very seriously, replying that it was too delicate a matter for a woman to discuss even in jest. Not until the sister knelt before her begging for pardon and promising that she would never mention it again, was Yü-hua appeased.

Later the inexperienced maiden related the incident to her brother, who, believing his wife guilty, decided to divorce her. He told Yü-hua that her father's servant had come for her, because her parents were seriously ill. He said he was too tired to go with her, and gave her a sealed letter—a document of divorce—to be taken home.

Wang felt better about the loss of his wife when it was reported that he had passed the imperial examinations. At the Chief Examiner's office he met the handsome Liu, who was being questioned repeatedly by the Examiner as to what noble deed he had done to win himself supernatural favour. After much thought Liu recollected and mentioned the pavilion incident, but he deemed it unworthy of being called a noble deed. Overhearing the conversation, the remorseful husband could do nothing but beg forgiveness of his ex-wife. The play ends with a happy re-union and the hasty wedding of Liu and Wang's sister.

Gramophone Records available:

Tan	by Mei Lan-fang	(梅 蘭 芳)		*Pathé*
„	„	„		*Odeon*
„	„	Chêng Yen-ts'iu	(程 硯 秋)	*Beka*
„	„	Hsu Pih-yuin	(徐 碧 雲)	*Odeon*
Lao-shên	„	Ma Lien-liang	(馬 連 良)	*Pathé*
„	„	Yen Chü-pêng	(言 菊 朋)	*Victor*
„	„	Kuan Ta-yüan	(貫 大 元)	*Odeon*
„	„	Wang Yu-ch'un	(王 又 宸)	*Beka*

THE SIGNIFICANT SASH

or HSIANG LOO TAI

（香 羅 帶）

General T'ang Tung's wife, Lady Lin, worshipped Lok, the private tutor of her son, because of his excellent personality and education. Her frequent praise of him displeased the general. One day T'ang was sent to Hangchow on some important business and that very night it happened that Lok had a high fever. The son, being very considerate, took his father's quilt and put it on the bed of his teacher and unintentionally his mother's specially-made sash was taken with the quilt.

On his return, T'ang became very angry when he discovered the sash on the tutor's bed. At the point of his sword he forced his wife to go to Lok. Bewildered at her husband's unreasonable order, she refused, but eventually the poor woman consented to knock on the tutor's door and plead for admission, because the general declared that he would kill both Lok and her, if she refused to obey his command. The young man not only severely reprimanded her, but left the place that very night. Though the wife's innocence was proved to T'ang, there was no opportunity to explain to Lok why Lady Lin had committed the indecent act of calling on him at midnight.

Sometime later, T'ang was ordered to subdue some pirates. To avoid all the official receptions on the way, he travelled incognito. It happened that he spent the night at a "Hê Tien" (literally, black shop) where the shopkeeper drugged his customers and then robbed them. When T'ang discovered the shopkeeper was a robber, he killed him and

259

intending to notify the local governor, he cut off the head (in olden times the killer often presented the head to the magistrate when he gave the information).

Before T'ang reached the court, one of his servants stopped him with the message that he must hasten to his destination.

The headless corpse gave rise to the misunderstanding that T'ang had been murdered, because T'ang's clothes and other things were found by the body. The magistrate, who happened to be Lok, the former tutor of T'ang's son, recollected the midnight incident and suspected that the wife was involved. The innocent woman was arrested. Recognizing the judge and feeling grief-stricken over her husband's death, she made a false confession of the murder of her husband and was sentenced to death. At the time set for execution T'ang hurried back, identified himself and brought about his wife's acquittal.

Gramophone Records available:

Tan . . . . by Sün Hui-shên　(荀 慧 生) . . . . *Odeon*

„ . . . . „　　　„　　　　　„　. . . . . *Beka*

SNOW IN JUNE

or LU YUEH HSÜEH

（六 月 雪）

NOTE I:—*Before the time of Emperor Ch'ien-lung* (A.D. 1736–1796) *the ending of this play was entirely different from what it is today. The story was as follows: Snow fell after Tou-ngê's execution in June, and for the following three years the land suffered a terrible drought. Not until the true culprit was found and executed did conditions return to normal. Emperor Ch'ien-lung felt dissatisfied with such an ending, because it failed to inspire the people with the thought that the good always prosper in the end. Therefore he commanded the playwrights to change to the present happy ending.*

NOTE II:—*There is yet another story concerning the change in the ending of this play: Since the Southern "hsi-wên"* (see Part I, Chapter V) *did not allow tragic endings, Tou-ngê's execution was replaced by the acquittal and, therefore, the play ends with the happy reunion of the hero and the heroine.*

Tsai, accompanied by Chang, the son of his woman-servant, left his mother and wife, Tou-ngê, and started for the capital to take the imperial examinations. Intending to take his beautiful mistress, Tou-ngê, to be his wife, Chang pushed Tsai into a river and returned home with the news that the young master had carelessly fallen into the river and been drowned. Grief made the aged mother very ill. In delirium she ordered Chang's mother to prepare some mutton broth. To get rid of the old mother, Chang poisoned the broth, but its odour was so strong that the patient would not even taste it. The smell, however, enticed Chang's mother, who gluttonously devoured the fatal dish and died almost immediately. Chang tried to force Tou-ngê to marry him, by threatening to prosecute her or her mother-in-law for murder. Her refusal resulted in the sick mother being dragged to the magisterial court.

Tou-ngê followed them there and seeing the judge torture her mother-law unjustly to force a confession—even a false one—she

261

sacrificed herself by asserting to the court that she was the murderess. Without investigating the matter to see whether her assertion coincided with the facts, the judge set the old woman free and much to Chang's disgust, convicted Tou-ngê of murder.

It is common to find only the climax or short interesting parts of a play given on the Chinese stage; except when performed by Ch'êng Yen-ts'iu (程 硯 秋), who has reconstructed the whole story, this play usually begins with the prison scene, in which the heroine sings to the jailor the story of her life. Then follows the street scene, the climax. (It was customary for the courts of olden times to parade those convicted of serious crimes on the main streets leading to the four gates of the city.) In this play, during the parade, the most pathetic and touching songs are sung. Tou-ngê prays Heaven to give her justice so that the wicked may be properly dealt with. Heaven answers her prayer by sending a heavy snowstorm—snow in June!—in the hottest month of the year (according to the lunar calendar).

This phenomenon compelled the Inspector-General to stop at this city and enabled Tou-ngê's neighbours to file a petition for a new trial. The past of the innocent prisoner was so clearly stated and proved that it was quite easy for the Inspector-General to see that a new trial should be granted.

Eventually Chang was executed and Tou-ngê acquitted. On her return, she was overjoyed to find her supposedly dead husband still alive. He had passed the imperial examinations! It was too much for her. It must be a dream! She was assured, however, by both her husband and mother-in-law that it was true. She was an Honoured Lady!

Gramophone Records available:

Tan	by Mei Lan-fang	（梅　蘭　芳）	Victor
„	„　　　„	„	Pathé
„	„　　　„	„	Great China
„	„ Ch'êng Yen-ts'iu	（程　硯　秋）	Beka
„	„ Tu Lee-yuin	（杜　麗　雲）	Great Wall
„ and Ch'ou	„ Mei Lan-fang		Victor
„ „ „	„ Hsiao Ch'ang-hua	（蕭　長　華）	„
„ „ „	„ Hsu Pih-yuin	（徐　碧　雲）	Pathé
„ „ „	„ Hsiao Ch'ang-hua		„
Lao-tan	„ Lee Too-ku'ei	（李　多　奎）	Beka
„	„ Wo-yuin-chu-shih	（臥雲居士）	Odeon

SPRING ROMANCE
or MOU TAN T'ING
(牡 丹 亭)

PART I. THE NAUGHTY MAID
or CH'UN HSIANG NAO HSŬÊ (春 香 鬧 學)

T'u Lee-nyiang, the beautiful and only daughter of a rich magistrate and Ch'un-hsiang, her vivacious maid, were studying under Professor Chên. The maid grew tired of studying, especially in spring, and one morning she persisted in playing all sorts of funny tricks on the old teacher, even after punishment. At last Chên was compelled to dismiss the class for the day.

She tempted her mistress to steal into the back garden.[1] Eager to see the flowers, now in full bloom, Lee-nyiang yielded to temptation.

PART II. THE DREAM BETROTHAL
or YOU YUAN CHING MÊNG (遊 園 驚 夢)

T'u Lee-nyiang re-arranged her hair and put on one of her best dresses as if she were entering a beauty contest with the flowers. After strolling in the garden for some time, the young maiden's heart became infatuated by the blossoms, the chattering birds and, above all, the spring air. She rested on the steps of the artificial hill and soon fell asleep. A handsome youth, holding a willow spray, came to woo her. She gladly gave him her heart, but alas, he was merely a spring dream!

Gramophone Records available:

Hsiao-shên..............by Yu Chên-fei   (俞 振 飛)................*Odeon*
Tan .... „ Shang Hsing-wu (項 馨 吾)................ „
„ .... „ Yüan Loo-an   (袁 蘿 盦)................ „
„ .... „ Shang Hsiao-yuin (尙 小 雲)................*Victor*

---

[1] The old custom was that young maidens were forbidden to play in the gardens in order to prevent them being seen by outsiders.

PART III. THE DREAM COMES TRUE
or HUAN HUN (還 魂)

When Lee-nyiang awoke, she was so disappointed that she died of a broken heart. As she had requested she was buried under a plum tree and her portrait, drawn by herself, was kept near the artificial hill.

Three years later while her father was in Yangchow, a young scholar by the name of "Liu" (meaning willow) came into this garden and happened to find the portrait, which he recognized as that of his dream sweetheart of one spring afternoon. He was so pleased that he put it on his bed. Again he dreamed of her and in this dream she asked him to dig open her grave, for, because he had found her, she was permitted to live again.

The next day Liu told his dream to a nun who took charge of the grave and they dug together. Behold, the maiden came to life again! The lovers started to Yangchow with the nun as their witness to inform Lee-nyiang's father of the resurrection and to seek his consent to their marriage.

The play, if all of it is given, ends with the happy marriage of the hero and heroine.

DATE:

A.D. 228

THE STRATEGY OF AN UNGUARDED CITY
or K'UNG CHENG CHI
(空 城 計)

During the period of the Three Kingdoms (A.D. 190-280) General Ma Shu (Illus. 87) of the Kingdom of Shu stupidly followed the saying, "Put oneself in a desperate situation to get salvation" by camping his men on the summit of a mountain. Of course, his shrewd enemy, Szŭ-ma I heavily beseiged him. Ma commanded his men to charge forward "to get salvation," but they failed. The result was the loss of the most strategic city, Chieh-t'ing. This loss enabled Szŭ-ma to march forward without resistance until he reached the headquarters of the Shu forces, where the commander-in-chief, Chu-kê Liang, camped.

Behold, the city-gates were wide open and two old soldiers were calmly sweeping near the gates! Chu-kê Liang, noted for his prudence, was seen drinking and playing on the "ch'in" (a musical instrument with seven strings) in the city-tower (see p. 25, Item 16) with only two servant-boys waiting on him. The music sounded so tranquil that Szŭ-ma could easily tell that the city was well protected by a hidden army, so he addressed Chu-kê Liang, "Though you are very clever, yet your trap does not catch me!" He then commanded his troops to retreat forty li (13-14 miles). Just as he was starting to set up camp, news came that the city was actually empty and that Chu-kê Liang had craftily opened the gates as a bluff. Szŭ-ma immediately returned, but it was already too late. A chance missed is lost forever! Reinforcements, headed by Chao Yuin, one of Shu's five "tiger" generals, had

Illus. 87. "Wu-ch'in" (by Hè Shou-ch'en in the Rôle of General Ma Shu)

PLAY: *The Strategy of an Unguarded City*

arrived. The city was no longer empty but well guarded! Szŭ-ma was defeated and more renown was gained by the great strategist of the Kingdom of Shu.

Gramophone Records available:

Lao-shên	....	by Yu Shu-yen	(余 叔 岩)	.... *Odeon*
”	....	” Yen Chü-pêng	(言 菊 朋)	.... *Great Wall*
”	....	” Wang Yu-ch'un	(王 义 宸)	.... *Odeon*
”	....	” ”	”	.... *Victor*
”	....	” Wang Shau-lou	(王 少 樓)	.... *Pathé*
”	....	” ”	”	.... *Beka*
”	and Ch'in	” Tan Hsiao-pei	(譚 小 培)	.... *Victor*
”	” ”	” Chia Fu-t'ang	(賈 福 堂)	.... ”
”	” ”	” Chang Ju-ting	(張 如 庭)	.... *Pathé*
”	” ”	” Kin Shau-shan	(金 少 山)	.... ”

Illus. 88.   1—"Tan" in· Fish-shaped Stocks (by Mei Lan-fang) ; 2—"Wên-ch'ou"
(by Hsiao Ch'ang-hua)

PLAY :   *The Extradition of Su San*

SU SAN, THE LOYAL SING-SONG GIRL

or SU SAN

(蘇 三)

PART I. THE EXTRADITION or SU SAN CH'I CHIEH (蘇 三 起 解)

Su San, a famous sing-song girl, was truly in love with one of her patrons, Wang Kin-lung, a rich young scholar, whom she often advised against wasting his money. Though much against the will of her mistress, she continued to advise him. After discovering that he had spent all his money, the mistress drove Wang out during Su San's absence. Upon her return, she traced him and succeeded in secretly supporting him so that he was able to go to Nanking to take the imperial examinations. At the farewell meeting, the girl and her lover vowed that neither would marry another.

Therefore, after his departure, Su San pretended to be ill and refused to accept any more visitors. This act offended the mistress so much that she secretly sold Su San as a concubine to a rich man in Hung-t'ung Hsien. She was told that her lover had passed the examinations, been made a great official, and had now sent for her to be his wife. She was overjoyed and started immediately for Hung-t'ung Hsien only to find that she had been betrayed. Grief made her really ill, so the ceremony had to be postponed. The jealous wife of the rich man, anxious to get rid of her before she became her husband's concubine, tried to persuade Su San to take some poisoned food which she prepared. As the poor girl felt too sick to eat anything, she left the food on the table. The unwelcome lover, coming to see her, happened to eat and was poisoned. The wife immediately accused Su San of murder and had her sent to prison. Furthermore, she bribed the magistrate who pronounced a death sentence on Su San.

In the meanwhile, Wang, the real lover, passed the examinations and became the head of the judges on that circuit. He was sent to the province in which Hung-t'ung Hsien was situated to investigate the criminal cases of that district. He was horrified to learn of the case against Su San. He at once sent for the prisoner. Part I starts with the arrival of the court officer at the prison to extradite Su San to Tai-yuan Fu, the capital city of the province, for re-trial. Though the officer assured her of a reversed judgment at the new trial, she still felt very gloomy concerning her future.

On the journey she told the officer her past history and how she had been cruelly tortured by the magistrate and his followers. This hard-hearted officer took pity on her, adopted her as his goddaughter and released her from the fish-shaped stocks (Illus. 88). He was greatly offended, therefore, when Su San remarked that none of the court men, from the magistrate down, were good. The clever girl immediately continued, "You, my godfather, are the only great man in the whole province!" Thus the officer was reconciled and permitted her to hide her bill of petition to the Chief Judge in the stocks so as to avoid the strict inspection of the magistrate. The journey scene lasts about forty minutes.

Gramophone Records available:

Tan . . . . by	Mei Lan-fang	(梅 蘭 芳)	*Beka*
„ . . . . „	„	„	*Pathé*
„ . . . . „	Ch'êng Yen-ts'iu	(程 硯 秋)	*Odeon*
„ . . . . „	Hsüeh Yen-ch'in	(雪 艷 琴)	*Beka*
„ . . . . „	Chang Ngê-yuin	(章 遏 雲)	*Great Wall*
„ . . . . „	Shang Hsiao-yuin	(尙 小 雲)	*Victor*
„ and Ch'ou . . . . „	{ Mei Lan-fang / Hsiao Ch'ang-hua	(蕭 長 華)	„
„ „ „ . . . . „	{ Mei Lan-fang / Ju Foo-hui	(茹 富 蕙)	*Great Wall*
„ „ „ . . . . „	{ Shang Hsiao-yuin / Ju Foo-hui	. . . .	„
„ „ „ . . . . „	{ Hsiao Ch'ang-hua / Hsu Pih-yuin	(徐 碧 雲)	*Odeon*

PART II. THE RE-TRIAL or SAN T'ANG HUI SHÊN (三堂會審)

Part II is a short one-act play with the court scene as its climax. In this scene, the actor playing the rôle of Su San sings the whole story of her life while kneeling. This is a very trying rôle, demanding an excellent voice and great endurance.

The play ends with the understanding that Su San is soon to be acquitted and that she will become the wife of the great judge, thus receiving the reward she so richly deserves.

The story of Su San is true and the court records of this case are still kept on file in the provincial court of Shansi. Her tomb is at the side of her husband's in the district of Yung-ning (永甯), Hopeh Province (河北省).

Gramophone Records available:

Tan	by Mei Lan-fang	(梅蘭芳)...........	*Victor*
„	„ Ch'êng Yen-ts'iu	(程硯秋)...........	„
„	„ „	„	*Odeon*
„	„ „	„	*Beka*
„	„ Shang Hsiao-yuin	(尚小雲)...........	*Odeon*
„	„ Sün Hui-shên	(荀慧生)...........	„
„	„ „	„	*Beka*
„	„ „	„	*Great China*
„	„ „	„	*Great Wall*
„	„ Hsu Pih-yuin	(徐碧雲)...........	*Beka*
„ and Shên	„ Mei Lan-fang and his troupe		*Pathé*
Hsiao-shên	„ Chang Miao-hsiang	(姜妙香)...........	„
Ch'ou	„ Ma Foo-lok	(馬富祿)...........	*Beka*

Illus. 89. Starting to Bury Flowers (by Mei Lan-fang)

PLAY: *Tai-yü at the Burial Mound of Flowers*

TAI-YÜ AT THE BURIAL
MOUND OF FLOWERS
or TAI YÜ TS'AUN HUA
（黛 玉 葬 花）

NOTE:—*This play, which Mei Lan-fang produced in 1915, is a selection from the immortal Chinese novel, "Hun Lou Mêng" (literally, the dream in the red chamber).*

Lin Tai-yü, the beautiful and clever heiress of Lin Ju-hai, was left an orphan at the age of fourteen, so she had no choice but to live with her maternal grandmother, Shih Tai-chun. Tai-yü was poetic, imaginative, highly emotional, and delicate in health. The wealthy old grandmother put her in an elaborate garden, called Tai Kuan Yüan (a name that has also become immortal in the literary world of China), with many of her cousins. A house, luxuriously furnished, together with a number of servants, was given to each of the charming maidens.

Chia Pao-yü, the much-spoiled grandson of Shih Tai-chun, was the only boy given the privilege of residing in this garden. Being a great admirer of the fair sex, he made the famous remark: "Boys are made out of dirty mud, while maidens are forms crystallized from pure water!" He not only enjoyed the company of his cousins, but was a devoted friend of all the pretty maidservants. He and Tai-yü were deeply in love with each other but as it was considered improper to reveal their real affection, neither of them could learn of the other's devotion.

The play opens here: Tai-yü awakes early one morning in late spring, in melancholy recollection of Pao-yü's refusal to see her the day before. In reality, Pao-yü had not refused to admit Tai-yü. One of his maidservants had thought the person knocking at the gate was a mischievous maid and so refused to let Tai-yü in. Absorbed in

273

jealousy and doubt, the latter, a born creature of moods, analogized herself, lonely and neglected, as the faded, fallen petals of the late spring flowers. In this mood of sympathy for the flowers she went out with a broom to gather the withered blossoms. Placing them in a bag, fastened to the tiny hoe which she bore on her shoulder (Illus. 89), she proceeded to a secluded corner of the garden where she had a mound built as the burial place of the withered blossoms. Here, Tai-yü, while meditating on who would bury her body in the event of her untimely death, mourned deeply over her own destiny as being even more sad than that of the blossoms.

It happened that Pao-yü also went to the burial mound of flowers and there met Tai-yü. Accusations and explanations ensued between the lovers, and the play ends in a happy reconciliation.

Gramophone Records available:

Tan . . . . by Mei Lan-fang   (梅 蘭 芳) . . . . *Pathé*
Hsiao-shên . . . . „ Chiang Miao-hsiang   (姜 妙 香) . . . . *Beka*

THE TALE OF THE LUTE

or P'I P'A CHI

(琵 琶 記)

NOTE:—*This is the masterpiece of the K'un-ch'u plays. Its composition is regarded as the cause of the revival of the Southern School in the Yuan Dynasty* (A.D. 1277–1368).

Ts'ai Yung, a brilliant scholar, only two months married to Chao Wu-nyiang, was urged by his father, much to his mother's disgust, to take the imperial examinations. Ts'ai refused to go to the capital on the grounds that his parents were old and that he must remain at home to support the family. Not until his old neighbour, Chang, promised to take good care of his family, did the filial son agree to leave for the examinations.

Ts'ai conducted himself so well through the examinations that he became the head of the literati. The Prime Minister admired him greatly and he was chosen to be his son-in-law. The young scholar refused the honour but was commanded by the Emperor to "marry into the Prime Minister's family."[1] Unable to help himself, Ts'ai sent a messenger home with some money, but the man he sent fled with the silver, and the message never reached his parents or his wife.

In the meantime misfortune overtook the family he left behind. Famine reduced them to starvation. Wu-nyiang sold her dowry to buy food for her parents-in-law. She herself had to eat bran so that the rice might last longer for the old couple.

---

[1] It is as customary in China for a man to marry into a girl's family as it is for a girl to marry into her husband's family. He is entitled to inherit his father-in-law's property as an heir.

Having observed that Wu-nyiang always ate by herself and in secret, the mother-in-law became suspicious that she was enjoying palatable food. Therefore, she hid herself one day in order to discover the secret. When she saw Wu-nyiang eating some dumplings, she rushed out and without close investigation, harshly rebuked her for her selfishness and demanded some of the dumplings. In spite of Wu-nyiang's refusal, she snatched the bowl. On discovering the truth, she shame-facedly devoured the bran mixture and was suffocated to death. The father-in-law, in deep grief, died almost instantly.

By this time Wu-nyiang had become so poor that she owned nothing that could be put on the market except her beautiful hair. While she was offering her hair for sale, Chang learned of her condition and gave her money to buy coffins. She felt too embarrassed to let Chang also pay for the burial, and started to raise the tumulus over the graves with her own hands. Being terribly exhausted, she fell asleep. When Chang's men came, genii had completed the mound for her.

Left all alone, Wu-nyiang decided to go to the capital to find her husband. She first painted portraits of her parents-in-law, and with these on her back and disguised as a Taoist nun, she sang ethical songs on filial piety to the accompaniment of the lute and thus earned her way to the capital.

Meanwhile Ts'ai, hearing no news from home, had to reveal the whole truth to his second wife, who immediately begged her father to let her visit her husband's home. The Prime Minister refused to grant her request, but consented to send a man to Ts'ai's home to fetch his parents.

Wu-nyiang reached the capital just as a big Buddhist celebration was going on. She sang and played on the lute so well that she earned money enough to pay for a memorial service to the parents-in-law. She hung the portraits and was just starting to worship when a high official came and frightened her so much that she hurriedly left without taking the pictures.

The official, Ts'ai Yung, recognized the portraits and tried hard to find the owner, but she had gone! He could do nothing but take the portraits home. When Wu-nyiang found out who the official was, she went to the front of his mansion to sing. The tale of the lute was overheard by the Prime Minister's daughter, who immediately sent for her. Not until she asked Wu-nyiang whether she had ever heard of the Ts'ai family in her native place and had expressed her sympathy for the deserted wife, did the wretched lady disclose her identity. Soon the two virtuous women became sisters.

The next morning Wu-nyiang was taken to Ts'ai's room where she found her lost portraits, on which she now wrote a poem, condemning Ts'ai as an unfilial son and a faithless husband. Ts'ai, however, was overjoyed to find the writer, and the play ends with a happy re-union.

Gramophone Records available:

Lao-shên ....by Lin Shŭ-shên （林 樹 森）................*Victor*

„ ....„ „ „ ....*Beka*

A TALE OF THREE DWARFS

or WŬ HUA TUNG

(三 矮 奇 聞 卽 五 花 洞)

Wu Ta-lang was an ugly dwarf, but his wife, P'an Kin-lien, was very beautiful. On account of drought in their native place, the couple started out for Yang-ko district to visit Wu's brother. It happened that two of the five mischievous rat-goblins were also travelling that way. They saw the ill-matched couple and desiring to cause another great disturbance among human beings, transformed themselves into the forms of Wu and Kin-lien. The four met. The wife could not feel certain which man her husband was, nor could Wu distinguish which woman was his spouse! They asked each other's name and found that they bore the same names! They began to quarrel, each accusing the other of being a hobgoblin. Finally, one of the group proposed to go to the magistrate and ask him to decide who was who.

Unfortunately, the magistrate was also a dwarf, so the puzzle became worse than ever. The case was then presented to Judge P'ao, who could tactfully decide all complicated cases even if the litigants were ghosts or goblins, for he could summon or dismiss them at will. He immediately sent for Chang, the Head of the Taoist Magicians, who owned among his priceless paraphernalia, a miraculous mirror, which, when raised before the goblin, would reveal its original form. Having discovered that the fake couple were two rats, Chang summoned the Cat God to arrest them. After many acrobatic stunts, the play ends with the capture of the goblins and the restoration of peace and public safety.

Gramophone Records available:

Tan ....by the "Four Kin-kongs" (see pp. 66-67):
      ⌈Mei Lan-lang (梅 蘭 芳)
      |Ch'êng Yen-ts'iu (程 艷 秋)
      |Shang Hsiao-yuin (尙 小 雲)
      ⌊Sün Hui-shên (荀 慧 生)..............*Great Wall*
 „ ....„ Chang Ngê-yuin (章 遏 雲)..............*Victor*

278

THE TRIAL OF LEE CHIH
or SHÊN LEE CHIH
(審 李 七)

Lee, a robber, after being arrested, decided to get revenge on his enemy, Wang, by falsely accusing him of being his accomplice in a recent robbery. When Wang came, the judge noticed that he was a scholar. Suspecting that Lee had been bribed to drag in Wang, he put the latter among his court attendants and ordered Lee to pick out his accomplice. Though Lee could not remember Wang's features clearly, it having been more than three years since Wang had insulted him, he half by threat and half by reprimand succeeded in discovering that one of the attendants was trembling; he pointed to him and alleged that the white silk now on Wang's legs was a part of the spoils they had robbed, for he recollected that Wang liked to bind his legs with white silk bought from a particular silk store, which he had once ransacked.

Deeming the evidence sufficient to prosecute Wang, the magistrate threw the scholar into prison. Unable to stand the torture, Wang was forced to make an untrue confession, which led to his conviction, just as the rascal had wished.

Not until the broken-hearted speech of Wang's grieving wife pierced his conscience did Lee confess the whole truth and thereby effect Wang's acquittal.

Gramophone Records available:

Ch'in .by Kin Shau-shan　(金 少 山) . . . .*Odeon*
　„　. . . . .„　　　　„　　　　„　. . . . .*Beka*

Illus. 90. On Board Ship. The Open Hand; "Tan" (by Mei Lan-fang);
"Lao-shên" (by Wang Shau-t'ing)

PLAY: *The Valiant Fisherman and His Daughter*

Like Robin Hood, "The Men of the Green Forest" used to rob the rich to help the poor and avenge the wrongs done to the oppressed by the oppressors. In this group of outlaws were Siao Eng and his beautiful daughter, Kuei-ing. The former thought himself too old to continue such a wild life, so he and his daughter chose to live by fishing. They were very unlucky for the weather was dry and fish were scarce. Unjust taxation and cruel extortion by the tax collectors, however, continued as before.

One afternoon when Siao Eng was entertaining two of his old friends on his boat, the insolent tax collector came again. His exorbitant demands enraged the friends so that they insulted not only the collector but his master, the head of the Tax Bureau. A group of hired men was immediately sent to punish the old man, who, in spite of his age, gave them a well-deserved punishment just as if he had been again a "Green Forester." The magistrate was angry and punished the old man with forty lashes for not paying the tax in time and for insulting the tax collectors.

Greatly worried when her father did not return home on time, Kuei-ing started to look for him, and met him as he came limping homeward. Both became very bitter at the injustice of the magistrate (Illus. 45) and they decided to re-join the "Green Foresters." Before resuming the life of outlaws, they determined to rid the community of its enemies, so they crossed the river (Illus. 90) at midnight, and killed all the oppressors,—the magistrate, the head of the Tax Bureau and their followers.

Gramophone Records available:

Tan	by Shang Hsiao-yuin	(尙 小 雲)	. . . .	*Odeon*
Shên	„ Tan Foo-ing	(譚 富 英)	. . . .	*Victor*
„	„ Yu Shu-yen	(余 叔 岩)	. . . .	*Great Wall*
Tan and Shên . . . . „	{ Mei Lan-fang	(梅 蘭 芳)		
	{ Ma Lien-liang	(馬 連 良)	. . . .	*Pathé*
„ „ „ . . . . „	{ Mei Lan-fang			
	{ Tan Foo-ing		. . . .	*Victor*
„ „ „ . . . . „	{ Tan Hsiao-pei	(譚 小 培)		
	{ Wang Yuin-fang	(王 芸 芳)	. . . .	*Pathé*
„ „ „ . . . . „	{ Shang Hsiao-yuin			
	{ Wang Shau-lou	(王 少 樓)	. . . .	*Beka*
„ „ „ . . . . „	{ Yen Chü-pêng	(言 菊 朋)		
	{ Yuin Yen-hsia	(雲 艷 霞)	. . . .	*Victor*

WHAT PRICE LIFE ?

or CHO FANG TS'AO

（捉 放 曹）

On discovering that the Prime Minister, Toong Tso, was planning to usurp the throne, Ts'ao Ts'au decided to get rid of him. In order to carry out his plan he became one of Toong's followers and one day slipped into Toong's house to assassinate him with the "Precious Seven-star Sabre." Toong, seeing him in a mirror, asked, "What do you want?" "To offer you this precious sabre," replied Ts'ao. After examining the fatal weapon carefully, the Prime Minister realized that it was a rare sabre. Therefore, Ts'ao's intrigue was not discovered.

Later, however, when Toong showed his son-in-law the sabre, the latter declared that Ts'ao's intention was to assassinate him. Soon, this remark was verified by Ts'ao absconding. His picture was hung at the city-gates and a reward was offered for his arrest.

One day, Chen Kung, the magistrate of Chung-mou district, received the report that Ts'ao had been arrested. When the prisoner was brought before him, his eloquence was such that he succeeded in convincing the magistrate that an attempt to assassinate the intending usurper was no crime and that he must join him in appealing to the loyal armies of the different provinces to overthrow Toong. Finally Chen gave up his post and followed his prisoner.

On their way they met Lu, a friend of Ts'ao's father, who insisted on their spending the night at his home. The host not only ordered his servants to kill a pig for the feast in honour of his guests, but went to the market himself to buy the best wine.

Hearing the sound of the sharpening of knives and finding Lu had gone out alone, Ts'ao began to suspect that the host had gone to report to the local officer in order to get the reward. In spite of Chen's remonstration, Ts'ao killed the whole family of the hospitable Lu. Not until he found the bound pig did he realize his suspicion was entirely unfounded. Of course, he and Chen had to flee. They happened to meet Lu returning. To Chen's great horror Ts'ao killed him too, on the pretext that he "preferred owing to being owed." (This saying is often quoted in ridiculing a selfish person, or, by changing the order of the words, one may boast of one's own virtue by saying, "I prefer being owed to owing".)

By the time they stopped at a tavern for the night, Chen very deeply regretted having become Ts'ao's friend. He planned to kill him, but lacking the courage to do so, he finally left the tavern alone before dawn.

Gramophone Records available:

Lao-shên	by Yu Shu-yen	(余 叔 岩)	*Pathé*
„	„ Wang Shau-lou	(王 少 樓)	*Victor*
„	„ Shih Hui-pao	(時 慧 寶)	„
„	„ Yen Chü-p'êng	(言 菊 朋)	*Great China*
„	„ Loo Hsiao-pao	(羅 小 寶)	„
„	„ „	„	*Odeon*
Lao-shên and Ch'in	⎧ Tan Hsiao-pei	(譚 小 培)	
	⎨ Tan Foo-ing	(譚 富 英)	
	⎩ Kin Shau-shan	(金 少 山)	*Beka*
„ „ „	⎧ Tan Foo-ing		
	⎩ Ger Kuei-sien	(婆 桂 仙)	*Odeon*

A WIFE'S SACRIFICE
or PAO LIEN TÊNG
（寶 蓮 燈）

Liu Yen-ch'ang, the magistrate of Luchow, had two sons, Ch'un-hsiang by the first wife, and Ts'iu-êrh by the second wife, Wang Kuei-ing. The boys loved each other devotedly and studied in the same school. While at school, one of their classmates named T'sin, the spoiled son of the Prime Minister, played a mean trick on the teacher. When the latter started to punish him, Ts'in rudely retaliated. Ch'un-hsiang to protect the teacher hit Ts'in with the ink-block and accidently killed him.

The boys went home and told their father about the accident, but Ts'iu-êrh with the intention of saving his brother, argued that it was he, not Ch'un-hsiang, who had committed manslaughter. Having failed to get the true facts the father asked his wife, Wang Kuei-ing, to help him find out who was the real perpetrator. The boys seemed to have agreed to give the same statements, so Kuei-ing was also thrown into great perplexity. From their different temperament, however,—Ch'un-hsiang gross, and Ts'iu-êrh refined—the parents suspected that the former was guilty. After much debate between Liu—partial to the motherless child—and Kuei-ing, mother of the delicate son, it was decided to send Ch'un-hsiang to a distant province and to make Ts'iu-êrh the prisoner.

Regretfully Liu took Ts'iu-êrh to the Prime Minister who, although insisting that the real culprit be found, ordered that Ts'iu-êrh be beaten to death, and that men be sent everywhere to search for Ch'un-hsiang.

Upon seeing Ts'iu-êrh thrown on the ground to be flogged, Liu plunged forward to cover the boy with his own body. He was "mercifully" thrown out and prevented from looking upon the cruel scene.

The senseless boy was believed dead and thrown outside the city where he was found by his parents who endeavoured to save his life. Their effort was discovered by the minister's men and all three of them were arrested.

Usually the play stops here, leaving the audience dissatisfied and eager to find out what became of the four miserable characters.

Gramophone Records available:

Tan . . . . by	Mei Lan-fang	(梅 蘭 芳)	*Victor*
„ . . . . „	Ch'êng Yen-ts'iu	(程 硯 秋)	*Beka*
„ . . . . „	Hsu Pih-yuin	(徐 碧 雲)	*Odeon*
Lao-shên . . . . „	Shih Hui-pao	(時 慧 寶)	*Pathé*
„ . . . . „	Yen Chü-pêng	(言 菊 朋)	*Odeon*
„ . . . . „	Wang Shau-lou	(王 少 樓)	*Beka*
„ . . . . „	„	„	*Great China*
Tan and Lao-shên . . . . „ ⎰ Mei Lan-fang ⎱ Ma Lien-liang		(馬 連 良)	*Odeon*

DATE:

ABOUT 1100 A.D.

YANG YEN-HUI VISITS HIS MOTHER

or SZU LANG T'AN MOU

(四 郎 探 母)

In the eleventh century during the Sung Dynasty (A.D. 960-1277) one of the northern tribes, which the Chinese contemptuously called the "Fans" became so aggressive that an expedition was sent by the Sung Emperor. At the head of this expedition were Yang Chi-yeh and his seven valiant sons, nicknamed the "Eight Tiger Generals." In the fatal battle at Kin Sha T'an, through betrayal by one of his own men, the old man lost his three eldest sons on the battlefield, and his fourth son, Yen-hui, was taken prisoner by the Fans. He was so handsome that he won the heart of the Fan Empress Dowager (Illus. 27) who even condescended to marry her beautiful daughter, the Princess of the Iron Mirror (Illus. 91) to the war captive.

For fifteen years he lived there incognito until one day he learned of his mother and brother's expedition to the north to fight against his adopted country. At the thought of their being so near and yet so inaccessible, he could not help lamenting his ill fate. The play opens here when his sentiments were being detected by the Princess, who continued inquiring and guessing until she discovered what the trouble was. Before she was told the whole truth, she was requested to swear secrecy, which she did. Love for her husband made her so bold as to

Illus. 91. The Mandarin Style of Dress (by Mei Lan-fang in the
rôle of the Princess of the Iron Mirror).

trick her mother and procure the Mandate Arrow (see p. 23, Item 2), the symbol of authentic power, with which the bearer might pass the border without obstruction. In the presence of the Empress Dowager, she pinched her child which she held in her arms. Its painful cry made the old lady curious. When questioned, the Princess said that the child wanted to play with its grandmother's royal Mandate Arrow and hence according to law, should be executed at once. Like any indulgent grandmother, the Empress Dowager ordered the law to be set aside and the child was given the Arrow, but with instruction that it must be returned before daybreak.

With the Arrow, Yen-hui hurriedly crossed the border and was captured as a spy sent by the Fans. His captor, Yang Tsung-pao, a young lieutenant serving on sentry, was his fourteen-year-old nephew. He was immediately taken to the father general, Yang Yen-chao. No sooner had the latter discovered the identity of the captive, than he shared his joy with the rest of his family by taking the brother to the inner camp to meet his mother, sister and the supposed widow of the long-lost general.

The happy re-union was a very short one. It was long after midnight when Yen-hui remembered the oath he had taken before the Princess that he would return before dawn. In the midst of great pleading by his family, a heart-broken parting ensued. But alas, he returned too late! The Fans were well prepared to arrest him, because the Empress Dowager had discovered her daughter's trick and had ordered an immediate arrest of the disloyal son-in-law. He would have been executed, had the Princess not played another clever trick on the old lady. At first the mother turned a deaf ear to the favourite daughter's pleading even when she said, "On whom shall I lean if you kill my husband? As a good horse never submits to a second set of harness, so a chaste woman never married twice." Then she recollected how she had obtained the Arrow through the darling child, so she again used her child to procure her husband's release. She threw the child into her mother's arms and feigned to commit suicide by the sword. The mother was again deceived and Yen-hui was released. Almost immediately, the solemn atmosphere was changed into one of lightness and gaiety by the mischievous Princess' three graceful "Ts'ing-an"[1] to appease the still dissatisfied mother.

Gramophone Records available:

Tan . . . . by	Mei Lan-fang	(梅 蘭 芳)	*Beka*
„ . . . . „	Chên Tê-lin	(陳 德 霖)	„
„ . . . . „	Ch'êng Yen-ts'iu	(程 硯 秋)	*Victor*
„ and Lao-shên . . . . „ {	Mei Lan-fang		
	Ma Lien-liang	(馬 連 良)	*Odeon*
„ „ „ . . . . „ {	Hsüeh Yen-ch'in	(雪 艷 琴)	
	Tan Foo-ing	(譚 富 英)	*Beka*
„ „ Ch'ou . . . . „ {	Mei Lan-fang		
	Hsiao Ch'ang-hua	(蕭 長 華)	*Victor*
Lao-shên . . . . „	Tan Hsiao-pei	(譚 小 培)	*Great China*
„ . . . . „	Yen Chü-pêng	(言 菊 朋)	*Odeon*
„ . . . . „	„	„	*Beka*
„ . . . . „	Wang Yu-ch'un	(王 又 宸)	*Victor*
„ . . . . „	Wang Shau-lou	(王 少 樓)	*Great China*
„ . . . . „	„	„	*Pathé*
„ . . . . „	Ma Lien-liang	(馬 連 良)	*Odeon*
Lao-tan . . . . „	Lee Too-ku'ei	(李 多 奎)	*Great China*
„ . . . . „	Wo-yuin-chü-shih	(臥 雲 居 士)	*Victor*
Hsiao-shên . . . . „	Chiang Miao-hsiang	(姜 妙 香)	*Odeon*

---

[1] "Ts'ing-an" is a peculiar kind of Manchurian bow performed by the women of that country.

Index

$\mathcal{I}ndex$

Titles of Plays in Italics